SPELLING MATTERS TOO

Jim Hildyard and Mark Morris

www.heinemann.co.uk

✓ Free online support
✓ Useful weblinks
✓ 24 hour online ordering

0845 630 22 22

Part of Pearson

CONTENTS

UNIT 6:
COMMON ENDINGS

UNIT 7:
SPELLING AND PUNCTUATION

UNIT 8:
MISC-SPELL-ANEOUS!

UNIT 9:
THE SPELLING CHALLENGE

Introduction

Spelling Matters Too is an engaging and flexible series that is designed to improve students' spelling skills. Each unit in the Student Book includes:

- **Objectives:** outlining the aims of the unit from the outset
- **Rules:** providing clear explanations and examples of the fundamental spelling rules
- **Danger:** warnings about any exceptions to spelling rules
- **Activities:** including a wealth of short and engaging spelling activities, as well as peer- and self-evaluation opportunities
- **Handy hints:** additional useful information to help students improve their spelling
- **Self-tests:** enabling students to check their own progress.

Diagnostic approach

The diagnostic approach means students can work independently to identify their own spelling weaknesses and then turn to the relevant teaching to address this. Students should complete the tests in Unit 1 and then use the analysis on pages 103–109 to direct them to the units they need to work through.

Also available for Spelling Matters Too

Your teacher may also have:

- **Spelling Matters Too Teacher Resource File**
Containing a wealth of worksheets, spelling games and additional self-tests. Also included is a CD-ROM containing editable Word files of the Teacher Resource File, ideal for customising.

- **Spelling Matters Too Interactive CD-ROM**

A suite of activities for use on an Interactive White Board that match the contents of the Student Book and bring spelling to life.

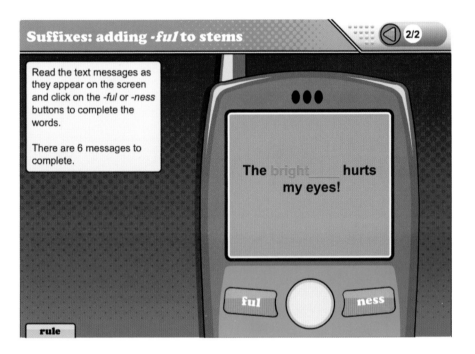

Look out for the icon in the Student Book, which lets you know when an interactive activity is available on the CD-ROM.

SPELLING STRATEGIES

Spelling strategies help you to look closely at words and give you ways of remembering how to spell them. In this unit you will:

- learn many strategies or ways to look at words and improve your spelling
- test your own spelling to find out what kinds of words you can spell well and where you need more help.

Look, say, cover, write, check

The five steps below will help you learn how to spell any word. They use sight, sound and memory to help you spell a word you may not have seen before.

1 LOOK
Look at the word for ten seconds.

2 SAY
Say the word to yourself.

3 COVER
Cover up the word when you feel you have learned it.

4 WRITE
Write the word from memory.

5 CHECK
Check your word against the original. Did you get it right? If not, what did you get wrong? Spend time learning that bit of the word. Go through the steps again until you get it right.

Activity 1

Choose one of the words below or a word you know you often spell wrongly. Use the five steps above to make sure you can spell it correctly.

| separate | independent | amount |

Activity 2

Read the article below. There are some difficult words to spell. Challenge yourself and use the LOOK, SAY, COVER, WRITE, CHECK steps to learn at least three of them.

Moonstruck astronaut believes in aliens

'I happen to be privileged enough to be in on the fact that we have been visited on this planet and the UFO phenomenon is real,' a former astronaut said on British radio last week.

'It has been covered up by governments for quite some time now,' added the astronaut, who grew up in Roswell, New Mexico, the location of the controversial 1947 incident in which some believe the US military covered up the crash scene of an alien spacecraft.

Activity 3

The extract below contains fifteen of the most commonly misspelled words in English. How many can you spell? Team up with a partner and use the LOOK, SAY, COVER, WRITE, CHECK steps to learn them.

I do an **unusual amount** of **exercise** before a fight: up to **eight** hours a day are **necessary**. My **friends** think I'm mad. On some **occasions**, like when there's a **competition** on, I **immediately** start a **different** routine, **beginning** with a **separate** training session before breakfast, which lasts two hours. It makes a **noticeable** difference and I **sincerely believe** it helps make me stronger before I enter the ring and beat some bad boy up.

Activity 4

Look back through your own work in English over the last few weeks. Find three words you often spell wrongly. Use the LOOK, SAY, COVER, WRITE, CHECK steps to help you learn the correct spelling.

Dictionaries and spell-checkers

Activity 1

You can use a dictionary to help you spell words correctly.
Dictionaries follow the order of the alphabet for grouping words.
The guide words at the top of each page show you the first and
last word on that page. Read the notes below from a dictionary.

guide word for first entry on the page

page number

word

type of word, for example:
n. = **noun**,
adv. = **adverb**.

second definition, used if a word has one or more meanings

guide word for the last entry on the page

definition

indicates origin of a word

guide to pronunciation

174

dead end   **debt**

dead end *n.* 1. road or passage with one end closed. 2. situation where there is no chance of making progress.
dead heat *n.* race in which two or more winners finish exactly together.

dearth (say derth) *n.* scarcity [from dear (*because scarcity made food, etc., expensive*)].
death *n.* dying; the end of life [from Old English].

deal *n.* 1. agreement or bargain. 2. someone's turn to deal at cards.
dear *adv.* 1. loved very much. 2. polite greeting in letters [*Dear Sir*]. 3. expensive.

debris (say deb ree) *n.* scattered fragments or wreckage.
debt (say det) *n.* something that you owe someone.

You might find that it helps the 'flow' of your writing if you finish your work
before looking in a dictionary to check any words you think you may have
spelled wrongly.

Activity 2

How do you quickly find two words in a dictionary that start with the same
letter? First, find the letter that the word starts with. The words are then listed
in alphabetical order by the rest of the letters in that word. For example:

2nd letter	3rd letter	4th letter	5th letter
tank	thanks	thrash	telecom
tent	theft	three	telegram
tidy	think	thrill	telephone
toad	thought	throw	telescope
tune	thunder	thrust	television

List the following words in alphabetical order.

tooth   task   tired   teeth
throw   tight   tall   table
tangle   three

Activity 3

Try this alphabetical challenge. First, choose a level.
The higher the level the more difficult the task. Then
place the words listed in that level in alphabetical order.

Level 1

ham   team   eat   any   self   fat   bat   peel   deep   jug

Level 2

mystery   light   exist   clear   multiply   button   burn   leader   orbit   alert

Level 3

half   hand   hammer   Halloween   hag   happy   hairy   hazard   habit   harp   hard

Activity 4

Write out this passage correctly:

> I wonder weather a spell
> chequer can fined the words
> witch I've spelled wrong?

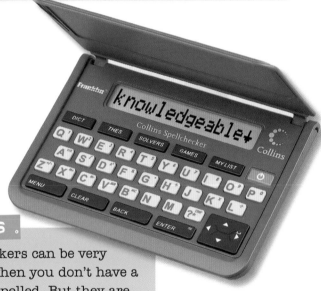

HANDY HINTS .

Handheld spell-checkers can be very
useful. These help when you don't have a
clue how a word is spelled. But they are
not perfect, as the extract below shows.

Peer-evaluation

For these tasks, work in pairs to test your partner's skills.
1   Use a dictionary to select ten words.
2   Ask your partner to place the words in alphabetical order.
3   How many words can you think of that come between **cure** and
    cut in the dictionary? List as many words as possible, then compare
    your list with your partner's. Who came up with the most?
4   Proof-read the passage opposite and write it out correctly. Swap
    your passage with your partner. Have you both spotted all the
    mistakes?

They're know miss steaks in
this newsletter cause we used
special soft wear witch checks
yore spelling. It is mower or
lass a weigh too verify. How
ever it can knot correct arrows
inn punctuation ore usage: an
it will not fined words witch
are miss used butt spelled rite.
Four example; a paragraph
could have mini flaws but
wood bee past by the spell-
checker.

Mnemonics

Activity 1

Read the following mnemonics that a student used to remember spellings. If you have difficulty spelling these words, then learn the mnemonics.

> **HANDY HINTS**
>
> A **mnemonic** is a rhyme or saying that sticks easily in the mind. Use mnemonics to help you remember how to spell a word.

rhythm

Rhythm
Helps
Your
Two
Hips
Move

geography

George's
Elderley
Old
Grandfather
Rode
A
Pig
Home
Yesterday

separate
Sep**arate** is **a rat** of a word to spell!

hear
You can tell the difference between **here** and **hear** because **hear** has an **ear** in it!

Activity 2

How well do you understand mnemonics? Choose three words from the list below and make up mnemonics that help you to remember them. If you prefer, you could use words that you know you often spell incorrectly.

> necessary   occasion   theatre   because

Activity 3

Many people use mnemonics to spell difficult words. Ask around. Does anyone you know use useful or amusing mnemonics?

Saying words as they are spelled

Activity 1

Read the following article out loud. Pronounce the **k** when it is followed by **n**.

Knitting knows no limits

Your granny <u>knew</u> how to <u>knit</u> but who'd have <u>known</u> it would make a cool comeback? If you've got the <u>knack</u>, you can <u>knock</u> up an iPod sock, a scarf, a digital camera case or a <u>knockout</u> woolly hat in ... ooh a couple of weeks. Don't dare <u>knock</u> it if you haven't tried it. If you've got a hole in your <u>knickers</u> then <u>knuckle</u> down and use your <u>knitwear</u> <u>knowledge</u> to repair it. A few <u>knowledgeable</u> <u>knots</u> is all it takes. Go on get <u>knitting</u>!

Activity 2

Some words have letters that are difficult to hear. It can help you to spell the word if you change the way you say it to yourself. For example:

government	gov / ern / ment	say **gov**, **ern** and **ment**
Wednesday	Wed / nes / day	say **Wed** then **nes** then **day**

The following words have difficult parts that can be spelled more easily using this technique. Work out how you will pronounce them.

interesting	listen	February	ghoul

Breaking words into parts

RULE

When you say a word out loud, you can hear that it is made up of one or more beats or sounds called **syllables**. For example, **fabulous** has three beats, or syllables.

beat 1	beat 2	beat 3
fab	u	lous

It will help you spell a word if you break it into smaller parts.

Activity 1

Split the words on the right into beats or syllables. Write them out with a line between each beat. The first word has been done for you. Learn how to spell the words.

1 nervous = ner / vous	**2** obstruction =
3 fraction =	**4** sometimes =
5 different =	**6** beginning =

See Unit 4, page **37** for more on stem words.

Activity 2

Words can often be broken into the following parts. Look at the word **replayed** for example:

re   **play**   **ed**

prefix added to the front of a stem to change its meaning (play – **re**play)

stem word cannot be broken up further

suffix added to the end of a stem (play – play**ed**)

How many words can you make using the stem word **play** and the prefixes and/or suffixes on the right? For example, **outplay** and **playful**.

Prefixes	Stem	Suffixes
re		ful
dis		fully
mis	play	ing
inter		ed
out		er
over		

Compound words

Compound words are complete words made from two stem words, for example: **moonlight** (moon + light).

Activity 3

How many compound words can you make with the words below? For example, you can make **airport** and **football**.

air down over ball play fall eye sleep ball light ground
under door way port stream strong head foot brow

Letter patterns

Activity 1

Copy out the table below. Leave some space in each column to add more words later. The table shows letter patterns often used at the start, middle and end of words. Students often spell these letter patterns wrongly.

HANDY HINTS

Many words contain the same letter patterns. Recognising these patterns will help you to spell more words correctly. For example: en**ough**, c**ough**, r**ough** have the **ough** pattern at the end.

Word	Start patterns	Word	Middle patterns	Word	End patterns
guest	gu-	thief	-ie-	sight	-ght
physics	phy-	shallow	-ll-	beautiful	-ful
when	wh-	button	-tt-	apple	-le
wrote	wr-	winning	-nn-	rough	-ough
knot	kn-	horror	-rr-	stitch	-tch
exercise	ex-	sobbed	-bb-	vague	-gue

See Unit 5, page **50** for more on common letter patterns.

Activity 2

Look at the words below. Copy them into the correct columns in your table from Activity 1.

what	shu**tt**ing	wei**ght**	ach**ie**ve	**wr**ists
bund**le**	**gu**ile	**kn**ight	corrupt	wa**tch**
physical	trave**ll**er	fi**tt**er	ma**nn**ers	bo**bb**ed
vo**gue**	**ex**cept	chi**ef**	aw**ful**	tou**gh**

Activity 3

Think of other words to add to the table that use the same letter patterns. How many can you list?

Proof-reading

Always check your work for spelling mistakes. If you need to check how a word is spelled, use the LOOK, SAY, COVER, WRITE, CHECK steps to learn it.

With any piece of writing:

- read your work carefully and underline any mistakes
- use a dictionary to check any word you are unsure how to spell
- swap work with a partner and look for each other's mistakes
- use a spell-checker if you are working on a computer.

Activity 1

Look back at your recent English work. List the ten spelling mistakes you make most often. Learn how to spell these words using the LOOK, SAY, COVER, WRITE, CHECK steps.

Activity 2

This computer game box contains fifteen spelling errors. Proof-read to find the errors. Then write out the words correctly.

MONSTER TRUCK MAYHEM

Agression-action-and excitment

- Crazy vehicles and extrordinary manouvres
- Feirce racing battles against freinds in the online multiplay mode
- Acheive sucess by unlocking suprise levels and new incredable monster trucks
- Churn the beautifull wastelands of Monument Valley where disastarous crashes are all part of the fun.
- Rev the engine, feel the exstasy of speed. Grab the oportunities and negociate incredible tracks.
- Never the same lap twice

Peer and self-evaluation

With a partner
Swap your work from Activity 2 with a partner. Have they identified the fifteen spelling mistakes? Have they now spelled those words correctly? If they have spelled a word correctly, put a tick beside it. If they haven't, then put a cross.

On your own
Use a dictionary to ensure you have spelled all fifteen words correctly. Has your partner marked your work correctly?

A history of words

Activity 1

Read articles a–e about the history of the English language.

a

The English language has a huge variety of words, handed down, borrowed or created over more than 2000 years. And it is still expanding! In fact, about half of all English words come from languages other than Old English. English is a global language, spoken or used by an estimated one-third of the world's population.

b

In 1066 William the Conquerer led the Norman French to invade England. The French were in control, and words like **castle**, **prison**, **challenge** and **royal** all came from them.

d

Dr Samuel Johnson wrote the first real dictionary in 1755. Before this date people spelled words as they liked! His book contained more than 40,000 words and was enormous – nearly half a metre tall and half a metre wide. Words he didn't like were omitted – **bang**, **budge**, **fuss**, **gambler** and **shabby** were all thrown out!

c

The Vikings had a big influence on our language. They first invaded in 787 bringing common sense words like *get*, *take*, *husband* and *wife*.

e

Developing technologies bring hundreds of new words to the language. Twenty years ago no one would have understood words like **Internet**, **texting**, **joypad** and **digital downloads**.

Activity 2

Write down five key facts these articles tell you about the English language.

Activity 3

Think about other words that have recently entered the language. How many can you discover?

Did you know?

Look at the pie chart below, which shows words that came into English from other languages.

Greek
aerial
(of the air)
encyclopaedia
(rounded education)
alphabet
(first letters of Greek
alphabet: alpha and beta)

Norse (Viking)
blunder
(from blundra 'shut one's eyes')
ugly
(dreadful)
call
(from kalla – cry loudly)

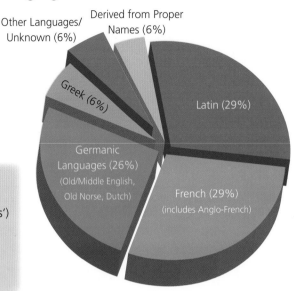

Other Languages/Unknown (6%)
Derived from Proper Names (6%)
Greek (6%)
Latin (29%)
Germanic Languages (26%)
(Old/Middle English, Old Norse, Dutch)
French (29%)
(includes Anglo-French)

Latin
wine
(from win)
annual
(from annus meaning year)
doctor
(teacher)

Norman French
crown
(from corune)
courtesy
(behaviour at court)
beef
(bull)

Activity 4

Many **prefixes** came into the English language from Greek. A prefix comes at the start of many different words and gives a clue to the meaning of a word.

> **tele** (means *far*) + scope (means *see*) = telescope
> Definition: A telescope is used to look at things that are far away
>
> **tele** (means *far*) + phone (means *voice*) = telephone
> Definition: A telephone carries voices long distances

See Unit 4, page 37 for more information on prefixes.

Write down three other words that use the prefix **tele**. Use a dictionary if you need help.

Peer-evaluation

The table below gives you a prefix (such as **micro**) and the meaning of the prefix (such as *small*). With a partner, copy out the table below and complete columns 3 and 4. Take it in turns to choose a prefix, fill in a word starting with the prefix and write its dictionary definition.

Greek Prefix	Meaning	Word found	Dictionary definition
anti	against		
auto	self	**auto**graph	
bio	life	**bio**logy	study of life
geo	earth		
hydro	water	**hydro**electric	
micro	small	**micro**scope	
mega	big		

New words

Technology brings us many new words. When new things are invented they need names. Many words enter the English language in this way. Often, inventors borrow from Greek and other languages.

> **nanobot** = *tiny robot*
> **nano** from greek (meaning *dwarf*)
> **bot** shortened form of robot from Czech **robota** (meaning *forced labour*)

Activity 5

What new inventions do you imagine will be around in the next 200 years? Invent four futuristic things, then dream up names for them. Put these names in alphabetical order with brief descriptions.

Activity 6

Copy out these words, which have entered the dictionary very recently. Can you find out what they mean?

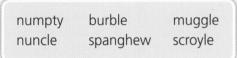

numpty	burble	muggle
nuncle	spanghew	scroyle

Activity 7

The Ancient Greeks did not use the letter **f**. Instead, they used **ph** – for example, **phone**. Many words in English use the **ph** letter pattern. Complete this quiz. All answers contain the **ph** pattern.

1 Use a camera to take one of these. __otograph
2 A mathematical diagram. gra__
3 A great victory or achievement. trium__
4 A section of a piece of writing. paragra__
5 A child with no parents. or__an
6 A round solid circular shape. s__ere
7 The letters from A through to Z. al__abet
8 Use to listen to a music player. ear__ones

Activity 8

List any more words you can think of that contain the **ph** letter pattern. Then make up a quiz like the one above to test a partner.

See Unit 5, page 55 for more on **ph** words.

Activity 9

Create a fact file that includes at least ten of the facts and figures you have learned. Use the title 'Words are history!' or make up your own title.

Diagnostic tests – Test your spelling

This unit has shown you many different strategies for improving your spelling. Now use these tests to find out what kinds of spelling you are good at and where you need more help.

Complete the tests below then turn to pages 103–109 to check your answers and find out where to go in the book for help.

Diagnostic test 1: Plurals

Write down the plurals of the following words. (Example: frame = frames)

1 frame	**11** reef	**21** cliff	**31** novelty	**41** criterion
2 wolf	**12** brick	**22** hamster	**32** policy	**42** inferno
3 hairbrush	**13** mouse	**23** county	**33** scruff	**43** shelf
4 bailiff	**14** journey	**24** thief	**34** bleach	**44** witness
5 banjo	**15** quality	**25** rodeo	**35** stress	**45** bakery
6 fireman	**16** bluff	**26** battery	**36** elbow	**46** scratch
7 belly	**17** fungus	**27** cable	**37** motto	**47** index
8 curtain	**18** tax	**28** person	**38** leaf	**48** design
9 apple	**19** foot	**29** piano	**39** trout	**49** casualty
10 picture	**20** strap	**30** crisis	**40** ceremony	**50** species

Now turn to page 103 for the answers and where to find help.

Diagnostic test 2: Spelling and punctuation

These sentences contain spelling and punctuation mistakes. Write each sentence out correctly. (Example: He heard his friend call, "See you in September, Tom.")

1 he heard his friend call, "see you in september, tom."

2 She wears out of date clothes but is a fun loving person.

3 Im not sure if its right. It doesn't look as if Ive done it properly.

4 All of the supporters shouting and cheering was extremely loud.

5 There was a programme about the raf on tv last night.

6 peter and sanjit went to a bonfire night display in york.

7 if i know marcia, i bet she knows the title of the new madonna cd.

8 There are alot of people who injure themselves running.

9 If Kellys there itll mean trouble. She doesn't get on well with Ellens friends.

10 they turned as he asked, "fancy coming to kfc? my treat? im feeling generous."

11 That doesnt belong to you. Im sure its davids.

12 only when he arrived in school did he remember about the french test.

13 When were there well make sure everythings ok.

14 If youre unsure about it, youd better check with emilys Dad.

15 "when the english play Australia, they always get thrashed," laughed shane.

Now turn to page 104 for the answers and where to find help.

Diagnostic test 3: Homophones and silent letters

Write out the following sentences using the correct spellings. (Example: Cheap fireworks are dangerous and should be banned.)

> **1** Cheep fireworks are dangerous and should bee band.
> **2** My lims ache but I don't now wether it's serious.
> **3** I drove passed the place where I past my driving test.
> **4** I used some sutle hints to sofen the news.
> **5** With a little more incite I wouldn't have needed a lone.
> **6** I'm sure your right, so I'll take your advice.
> **7** We kneed to decide wear to go next thyme.
> **8** If you have two much fatty food you may have too cut it down.
> **9** You're rong, so don't get your nickers in a twist!
> **10** Eye sore ewe walk threw that puddle.
> **11** Take your coat of. It's the middle of summer.
> **12** I wish I'd scene that knew film.

Now turn to pages 104 and 105 for the answers and where to find help.

Diagnostic test 4: Soft letter sounds

Write down the correct spelling. (Example: cemetery)

1 cemetery / semetery		**16** accomplice / accompliss
2 terrace / terriss		**17** cituation / situation
3 generate / jenerate		**18** engine / enjine
4 fanciful / fansiful		**19** gealous / jealous
5 dismice / dismiss		**20** currency / currensy
6 cegment / segment		**21** bandage / bandadge
7 sponge / sponje		**22** knowledge / knowlege
8 delicacy / delicasy		**23** cartrige / cartridge
9 specimen / spesimen		**24** apprentice / apprentiss
10 crevice / creviss		**25** cider / sider
11 dunce / dunse		**26** infancy / infansy
12 fireplace / fireplase		**27** gesture / jesture
13 decimal / desimal		**28** crucify / crusify
14 necklace / neckliss		**29** adhecive / adhesive
15 cynical / synical		**30** gymnastics / jymnastics

Now turn to page 105 for the answers and where to find help.

Diagnostic test 5: Common letter patterns

Write down the correct spelling. (Example: their)

1 their / thier	**16** recieve / receive
2 glacier / glaceir	**17** earphones / earfones
3 achieve / acheive	**18** review / reveiw
4 briefcase / breifcase	**19** shield / sheild
5 emphasis / emfasis	**20** fiend / feind
6 field / feild	**21** physical / fysical
7 trophy / trofy	**22** rephund / refund
8 sufficient / sufficeint	**23** wield / weild
9 concieve / conceive	**24** perceive / percieve
10 phunnel / funnel	**25** holograph / holograf
11 relieved / releived	**26** sliegh / sleigh
12 oriental / oreintal	**27** recievership / receivership
13 phase / fase	**28** briefing / breifing
14 hieght / height	**29** grievous / greivous
15 conscience / consceince	**30** viewer / veiwer

Now turn to pages 105 and 106 for the answers and where to find help.

Diagnostic test 6: Common letter patterns

Write down the correct spelling. (Example: mechanic)

1 mechanic / mekanic	**16** warmth / wormth	**31** clowt / clout
2 branch / brantch	**17** devowt / devout	**32** werth / worth
3 wrech / wretch	**18** fowndation / foundation	**33** wonder / wunder
4 gorgeous / gorgeus	**19** clishé / cliché	**34** scratched / scrached
5 powder / pouder	**20** maches / matches	**35** twitch / twich
6 shef / chef	**21** coutch / couch	**36** archive / arkive
7 wrench / wrentch	**22** chasm / kasm	**37** queer / qweer
8 approach / approatch	**23** squadron / sqwadron	**38** ineqwality / inequality
9 hownd / hound	**24** shauvinism / chauvinism	**39** sqweak / squeak
10 sheperd / cheperd	**25** shassis / chassis	**40** wardrobe / wordrobe
11 teacher / teatcher	**26** munch / muntch	**41** architect / arkitect
12 wand / wond	**27** bewiched / bewitched	**42** search / seartch
13 squat / sqwat	**28** anxious / anxius	**43** equator / eqwator
14 luxury / louxury	**29** dubious / dubius	**44** cownty / county
15 liqwid / liquid	**30** bownd / bound	**45** enqwire / enquire

Now turn to page 107 for the answers and where to find help.

Diagnostic test 7: Prefixes and suffixes

Write out the word and underline the **prefix**. (Example: <u>un</u>masked)

1	unmasked
2	undergrowth
3	preselect
4	immature
5	rediscover
6	overhead
7	misbehave
8	unnatural
9	antifreeze
10	disallow

Write out the word and underline the **suffix**. (Example: beaut<u>iful</u>)

11	beautiful
12	sharpest
13	fixing
14	battlements
15	priceless
16	darken
17	enjoyed
18	higher
19	happiness
20	dreaded

Write down the correct spelling. (Example: always)

21	allways / always
22	mispell / misspell
23	unnerve / unerve
24	ilegal / illegal
25	misspent / mispent
26	overreact / overeact
27	immaterial / imaterial
28	unoticed / unnoticed
29	irregular / iregular
30	imediate / immediate

Write down the correct **suffix**. (Example: dark<u>ness</u>)

31	dark (ness, ful, less)
32	night (ly, less, ness)
33	retire (ful, ment, less)
34	trade (ly, ed, ment)
35	demand (ly, ing, ment)
36	hope (ful, ly, ment)
37	exact (ous, ly, ful)
38	wind (ful, ment, ing)
39	hard (less, ness, ful)
40	carry (ing, ly, ment)

Write down the stem word and **suffix** correctly. (Example: forgiveness)

41	forgive + ness
42	victory + es
43	believe + ed
44	careful + ly
45	forgive + ing
46	easy + est
47	clue + less
48	nurse + ing
49	heavy + est
50	amuse + ed

51	carry + ing
52	ability + es
53	slob + ish
54	wet + er
55	chisel + ing
56	travel + ing
57	home + less
58	faith + ful
59	spiral + ing
60	grovel + ing

Now turn to page 107 for the answers and where to find help.

Diagnostic test 8: Word endings

Make a complete word by adding the correct ending.

Choose from '-tion', '-sion', '-ssion', '-cian' (Example: occa<u>sion</u>)

1	occa-	7	man-	13	depre-	19	tacti-
2	electri-	8	magi-	14	adora-	20	exhibi-
3	accelera-	9	aggre-	15	confe-	21	opti-
4	discu-	10	exclu-	16	beauti-	22	po-
5	posse-	11	pa-	17	physi-	23	dimen-
6	explo-	12	devo-	18	expan-	24	televi-

Choose from '-ous', '-ious', '-eous' (Example: nervous)

25 nerv-	**30** advantag-	**35** hid-	**40** myster-
26 ted-	**31** nutrit-	**36** anx-	**41** spontan-
27 jeal-	**32** gener-	**37** gorg-	**42** simultan-
28 courag-	**33** anonym-	**38** monstr-	
29 scrumpt-	**34** cur-	**39** poison-	

Choose from '-le', '-al' (Example: decimal)

43 decim-	**49** electric-	**55** anim-	**61** beet-
44 fin-	**50** accident-	**56** ped-	**62** fidd-
45 bott-	**51** ank-	**57** diabolic-	**63** cand-
46 purp-	**52** cryst-	**58** need-	**64** emotion-
47 manu-	**53** arriv-	**59** mirac-	**65** ming-
48 gigg-	**54** financi-	**60** logic-	**66** mechanic-

Choose from '-ate', '-ite' (Example: indicate)

67 indic-	**72** irrit-	**77** eradic-	**82** particip-
68 oppos-	**73** inv-	**78** celebr-	**83** demonstr-
69 imit-	**74** decor-	**79** altern-	**84** evapor-
70 termin-	**75** concentr-	**80** co-oper-	
71 rec-	**76** gran-	**81** navig-	

Choose from '-ical', '-icle', '-acle' (Example: musical)

85 mus-	**90** obst-	**95** ic-	**100** chem-
86 med-	**91** art-	**96** mathemat-	**101** barn-
87 mir-	**92** geograph-	**97** bibl-	**102** class-
88 veh-	**93** spect-	**98** tent-	
89 techn-	**94** phys-	**99** com-	

Choose from '-ance', '-ence' (Example: innocence)

103 innoc-	**107** audi-	**111** appli-	**115** depend-
104 dist-	**108** brilli-	**112** sci-	**116** insur-
105 coincid-	**109** evid-	**113** ambul-	**117** rom-
106 perform-	**110** experi-	**114** lic-	**118** gl-

Choose from '-able', '-ible' (Example: acceptable)

119 accept-	**122** afford-	**125** divis-	**128** compat-
120 understand-	**123** respons-	**126** flex-	**129** valu-
121 comfort-	**124** wash-	**127** prob-	**130** leg-

Now turn to pages 108 and 109 for the answers and where to find help.

Diagnostic test 9: Letter patterns

Choose the correct letter pattern to complete each word below.

(a) (ai) (ay) (ei) (ey) (ea)	
1 vehicle on tracks	= tr__n
2 hang around	= st__
3 orders in the army must be	= ob__ed
4 cargo on ship	= fr__ght
5 beef meat	= st__k
6 Jesus born in	= m__nger
7 smash something	= br__k

(e) (ea) (ee) (ie) (ei) (i)	
8 people working together	= t__m
9 to finish something	= compl__te
10 roof of a room	= c__ling
11 fetch something	= retr__ve
12 flesh of animal	= m__t
13 walk on these	= f__t
14 girl's name	= Paul__ne

(i) (y) (ie) (ye) (uy) (ey)	
15 similar to OK	= f__ne
16 Boy's name	= G__
17 say farewell	= goodb__
18 purchase	= b__
19 to colour clothes	= d__e
20 has pastry top	= p__
21 particular kind	= t__pe

(o) (oa) (ow) (ough) (ew)	
22 similar to frog	= t__d
23 scatter seeds	= s__w
24 opposite of fast	= sl__
25 skeleton made of	= b__nes
26 keeps above water	= fl__t
27 to stitch	= s__
28 bread made from	= d__

(u) (oo) (o) (ew)	
29 want something to…	= d__
30 summer month	= J__ne
31 impolite	= r__de
32 appears in night sky	= m__n
33 staff on a ship	= cr__
34 eat soup with	= sp__n
35 traveller to work	= comm__ter

(u) (ue) (ew) (eu)	
36 after Monday	=T__sday
37 melodious notes	= t__ne
38 school student	= p__pil
39 not many	= f__
40 female sheep	= __e
41 won't take sides	= n__tral
42 a continent	= __rope

Now turn to page 109 for the answers and where to find help.

WELL DONE! You have completed all the tests! Remember to check your answers against the charts on pages 103–109. You can also see where to turn in the book to make your spelling even better!

VOWELS AND CONSONANTS

OBJECTIVES

Letters are divided into *vowels*
(**a, e, i, o, u**, and sometimes **y**) and *consonants*
(other letters). In this unit you will:

- understand how vowels and consonants are used in words
- learn about long and short vowel sounds
  sh**a**de = long vowel sound   s**a**d = short vowel sound
- learn the different ways that long and short vowel sounds
  can be spelled.

RULES

The five vowels are: **a   e   i   o   u**

The rest of the letters in the English alphabet are consonants, but **y**
can be used as a vowel *and* a consonant.

- The letter **y** becomes a *vowel* when it sounds like:
  long **i** in wh**y**, sh**y**, short **i** in m**y**th *and* **e** in merr**y**, ver**y**
- The letter **y** is a *consonant* when it sounds like:
  y in **y**ear or **y**esterday

Activity 1

Vowels are very important. Look at the sentence below.
All the vowels have been taken away. Work out the
missing letters then write out the complete sentence.

> Th__ l__ng__st __nd h__gh__st r__ll__r c____ster
> __n the w__rld __s th__ St____l Dr__g__n in J__p__n.

Activity 2

Write out the complete words for the list below,
underlining the vowels you have added.

> snk   Plysttn 3   cmptr   ftbll

RULE

Vowels can sound **long** or **short**.

- A *long vowel* makes the same sound as when you say the vowel on its own:
  r**a**te   th**e**se   wh**i**te   fr**o**ze   am**u**se
- A *short vowel* doesn't make the same sound as when you say the vowel on its own:
  b**a**t   p**e**n   f**i**t   g**o**t   b**u**s

Short vowels

Activity 1

Write down the short vowel words you can make from the word wheels opposite. Each word must contain the vowel in the centre of the circle.

Activity 2

A short vowel sound is sometimes made from more than one vowel. The vowels that make the sound may be unexpected. Copy out the table below. Say each word, then put it in the correct vowel sound column.

short 'e' sound	short 'i' sound	short 'o' sound	short 'u' sound
as in t**e**n	as in t**i**p	as in t**o**p	as in t**u**b
h**ea**d	m**y**stery	bec**au**se	g**oo**d

s**ai**d	cr**y**stal	r**ou**gh	br**o**ther	t**ou**gh	c**ou**ld	l**e**sson	pl**ea**sure
t**oo**k	bag**ue**tte	w**a**s	ang**ui**sh	cr**y**pt	squ**a**bble	w**a**nder	fr**ie**nd

Activity 3

Write out the following review. Fill in the letters that make the short vowel sound.

Film review

Indiana Jones and the K_ngdom of the Cr_stal Skull

Rating: Very g_ _d

In a cr_pt in ancient Peru, Indy and fr_ _nds are b_sy keeping you on the edge of your seat. The plot sh_ _ld keep you g_ _ssing. A squad of zombies with missing h_ _ds makes for a pr_tty exciting opening. It's followed by enough brilliant action sequences to make your eyes pop out. Who s__d this fantastic series of films was d__d? Take your m_ther. She'll l_ve it.

Long vowels

- A **long vowel** sound can be made by a vowel on its own:

  m**a**ke   th**e**se   t**i**re   r**o**pe   h**u**ge

- A **long vowel** sound can also be made using two or three common letter patterns. For example, the long vowel sound **a** in t**a**ke can also be spelled:

  t**a**ke   tr**ai**n   tr**ay**   th**ey**

Learning these common patterns will help you to spell more words correctly.

Long vowel sound 'a'

Activity 1

Copy the table below. It shows you which letter patterns make the long vowel sound 'a' and how common they are. Leave extra room to add more words.

Letter patterns that make the long vowel sound 'a'

Letter pattern	a (often)	ai (often)	ay (often)	ei (not often)	ey (not often)	ea (not often)
Example	f**a**de	m**ai**d	del**ay**	fr**ei**ght	th**ey**	br**ea**k

Activity 2

Read the brochure below. Put the words with the long vowel sound 'a' into the correct column of the table you made in Activity 1.

Vegetarian tigers: no miss steak

Fancy t**a**king an unusual br**ea**k? Why not explore the depths of the jungle? If you want to go aw**ay** on holid**ay** to Thailand, then m**a**ke a visit to the f**a**mous Tiger Temple. Here you'll find t**a**me tigers on displ**ay**. These gr**ea**t beasts pl**ay** with the visitors, pose for photographs and most am**a**zing of all – th**ey** don't eat meat! Don't be afr**ai**d; create a wonderful trip. Choose from **ei**ght diffferent travel options and create a t**ai**lor-m**a**de holiday. Don't del**ay**! Book now on 0222 101010

GIVE
PEAS
A CHANCE

Activity 3

Write your own exciting adventure holiday brochure using words that contain the long vowel sound 'a'. Try to use each way of spelling the vowel sound 'a' at least once.

Long vowel sound 'e'

Activity 4

Copy out the table below. It shows you which letter patterns make the long vowel sound '**e**'.

Letter patterns that make the long vowel sound 'e'

Letter pattern	e (often)	ea (often)	ee (often)	ie (not often)	ei (not often)	i (not often)
Example	th**e**	dr**ea**m	wh**ee**l	gr**ie**f	dec**ei**ve	magaz**i**ne

Activity 5

Read the article opposite. Put the words with the long vowel sound **e** into the correct column of the table you made in Activity 4.

The Stee**l Dragon: a dr**ea**m machine**
We f**ee**l that th**e**se days it s**ee**ms hard to scare anyone. But a t**ea**m in Japan have created th**e** largest and highest rollercoaster in the world…and it's called The St**ee**l Dragon. Once you've b**ee**n mad enough to get aboard you'll sw**ee**p down into crazy ravines, experience w**ei**rd loops and scr**ea**m with the terror of b**ei**ng almost 100 metres in the air. It's a terrific f**ee**ling when you've ridden it; what an ach**ie**vement!

Long vowel sound 'i'

Activity 6

Copy out the table below. It shows you which letter patterns make the long vowel sound '**i**'.

Letter patterns that make the long vowel sound 'i'

Letter pattern	i (often)	y (often)	ie (not often)	ye (not often)	uy (not often)	ey (not often)
Example	m**i**ne	h**y**pe	p**ie**	d**ye**	g**uy**	**ey**esight

Activity 7

Read the following headlines. Write the words with the long vowel sound '**i**' into the correct column of the table you made in Activity 6.

Man wins prize in pie eating contest

Chart delight as pop star shines bright

Hype and lies over UFOs seen flying in the sky

Boxer shows true might on fight night

Billion pound buy for fine wine collector

Big fines for speeding crimes deter boy racers

Not a dry eye in the house on first night

Peer-evaluation

On your own
Write some headlines of your own. Try to include as many long vowel '**i**' words as you can.

With a partner
Swap your headlines with a partner and compare your lists. Who wrote the most headlines? Who included the most words containing the long vowel sound '**i**'?

Long vowel sounds 'o' and 'u'

Activity 8

Copy out the table below and learn the letter patterns.

Letter patterns that make the long vowel sound 'o'

Letter pattern	o (often)	oa (often)	ow (often)	ough (not often)	ew (not often)
Example	go bone explode phone	toad unload approach soaked	below low throw show	though although	sew

Activity 9

The long vowel **u** can sound like **oo** (r**u**de), or **yoo** (c**u**be).

Copy out the tables below and learn which letter patterns make each sound.

Letter patterns that make the long vowel sound 'u' as in blue

Letter pattern	u (often)	oo (often)	o (often)	ew (not often)
Example	blue	moon	move	crew

Letter patterns that make the long vowel sound 'u' as in cube

Letter pattern	u (often)	ue (not often)	ew (not often)	eu (not often)
Example	tune	fuel	new	feud

Write the words below into the tables you made.

Make sure you put them in the correct place according to their letter pattern.

due	June	who	ruby	brew	move	strewn	tube	soothed	spoon	food
too	crew	blew	lose	mood	do	improved	loot	groove	rude	clue

Activity 10

Find the words with the long vowel sound **'u'** in the sentences below.

Write the words you have found into the tables in Activity 9.

- The confused pupil couldn't work his new computer.
- There was a bright new crescent moon in the sky overhead.
- At Tuesday's match there were very few neutrals in the crowd.
- I can't afford to renew my membership to the snooker club.
- I would argue that that referee's decision was dubious.

Vowels and consonants: self-tests

Complete the tests below. When you have finished, your teacher will have the answers to check against.

Self-test

Write down whether each word has a long vowel sound or a short vowel sound.

1 f**u**zz

2 t**ea**ch

3 b**i**n

4 ch**ai**n

5 wh**y**

Self-test

Write down which long vowel sound is made by the letters in bold.

1 I feel gr**ea**t.

2 I can't stop sn**ee**zing.

3 That's a brilliant new t**u**ne.

4 Have you had a flu vacc**i**ne?

5 I prefer beer to w**i**ne.

Self-test 3

Choose the correct letter pattern for each gap from those given in bold above the clues.

Long vowel sound 'a' **a ai ay ei ey ea**	
1 not genuine	f_ke
2 race in a team	rel_ _
3 mucky mark	st_ _n
4 follow orders	ob _ _
5 destroy object	br _ _ k
6 shipping cargo	fr_ _ ght

Long vowel sound 'e' **e ea ee ie ei i**	
7 very tidy	n _ _ t
8 bed covering	sh _ _ t
9 trick somebody	dec _ _ ve
10 succeed	ach _ _ ve
11 finished	compl_te
12 woman's name	Paul _ ne

Long vowel sound 'i' **i y ie ye uy ey**	
13 use to colour hair	d _ _
14 expression of sadness	s _ gh
15 hole in a needle	_ _ e
16 aeroplanes fly in the	sk _
17 man's name	G _ _
18 apple...	p _ _

Long vowel sound 'o' **o oa ow ough ew**	
19 basis of bread	d_ _ _ _
20 transport on water	b _ _ t
21 chuck something	thr_ _
22 something said	sp _ ken
23 stitch clothes	s _ _

Long vowel sound 'u' (oo, as in rude) u oo o ew	
24 popular at parties	ball_ _n
25 not false	tr _ e
26 men on board ship	cr _ _
27 opposite of don't	d_

Long vowel sound 'u' (yoo, as in tune) u ue ew eu	
28 heated discussion	arg _ ment
29 instead of something	in li_ _
30 music download software	iT _ nes
31 not so many	f _ _

29

PLURALS

This unit will help you to spell *plural* words correctly. By the end of this unit you will:

- know the many ways to turn singular words into plurals
- spell plural words correctly.

When to add 's' or 'es'

RULES

- The most common way to make a word plural is to add **s**. For example:

    road → *road**s***   *sweet* → *sweet**s***   *frog* → *frog**s***

- But there are times when you will need to add **-es** to make a plural. If a word ends in **s**, **sh**, **ch**, **x**, or **ss** remember to add **-es** to make it plural:

    witch → *witch**es***   *wish* → *wish**es***   *tax* → *tax**es***

- You can hear an **-es** plural because it adds another *syllable* to the word. Look at these examples:

    *flash (**one syllable**)* → *flash/es (**two syllables**)*
    *ad/dress (**two syllables**)* → *ad/dress/es (**three syllables**)*

HANDY HINTS

Singular means there is only one: for example, a book.
Plural means more than one: for example, three books.

Activity 1

Read the magazine article below. Write out the words in blue in their plural form.

Recent **month** have seen increasing **number** of **clash** between concerned **group** of **parent** and the **manufacturer** of computer **game**. **Hundred** gathered at **meeting** throughout the UK this week, and heard passionate **speech** from those who believe the **hour** that **teenager** spend playing on their **console** should be strictly limited. Some **supporter** argued that staring at **monitor** can cause various **illness** and called for radical **approach** to the problem. "It's the tiny **screen** that are doing the damage," claimed Dr Pamela Harrison. "Young **kid** are playing on their **phone** far too much. The **button** and **switch** they have to use are putting an unnecessary strain on the **eye**." A statement for the Electronic Gaming Association responded by pointing out that clear **warning** about the **danger** of excessive use are clearly printed on **box**, **instruction** and the software itself.

Activity 2

Read the interview below. Write out the words in blue in their plural form.

British motor racing star Chris Hildrew added to his list of **triumph** at the weekend. Following the race he spoke enthusiastically to **reporter** about the victory.

"The whole thing just went brilliantly today. Following those **stroke** of bad luck in the last two **race** I was delighted there were no **hitch** and **thing** went smoothly. After the first few **corner** I was already three **second** ahead and I just put my foot to the floor, without putting any **stress** and **strain** on the suspension. The only **problem** I faced came nearer the end, when lapping the **driver** at the back. It can sometimes be tricky getting past **bunch** of the slower moving **car**. I'm optimistic for the Championship now. After seven podium **finish** in a row, I've got to fancy my **chance** for the title."

DANGER

One of the most common spelling errors that people make involves plural words. It is a mistake to add an apostrophe before an **s** when you only mean the word to be plural.

He owns two dogs ✔
NOT
He owns two dog's ✘

The lights were on ✔
NOT
The light's were on ✘

Simple plural words **DO NOT** need an apostrophe.

I fancy some chips ✔
NOT
I fancy some chip's ✘

See Unit 7, page 83 for more on apostrophes

Self and peer-evaluation

On your own

Read the magazine article about computer games on page 30 again. Write a response to that article. You must include the plural form of the following words:

| friend | teacher | argument | hour |

| wish | computer | skill |

With a partner

Swap your response with a partner. Have they correctly written down the plurals? Make a note of any plural words you think they have spelled incorrectly.

Words ending in 'f', 'ff' or 'fe'

RULES

- Any words that end in **ff** need an **-s** to make them plural, for example:

    bailiff ➔ *bailiff**s**   *bluff* ➔ *bluff**s***

- Words that end in **f** or **fe** are trickier. Some are made plural by adding **-s**, such as:

    proof ➔ *proof**s**   *roof* ➔ *roof**s***

- Other words ending in **f** or **fe** change the **f** to **v** and add **-es**, such as:

    life ➔ *li**ves**   *wolf* ➔ *wol**ves***

- Some words that end in **f** can be spelled with either an **-fs** or a **-ves** plural ending, such as:

    scarf ➔ *scarf**s** or *scar**ves***
    dwarf ➔ *dwarf**s** or *dwar**ves***
    handkerchief ➔ *handkerchief**s** or *handkerchie**ves***

HANDY HINTS

There is no clear rule for spelling the plural form of a word ending in **f** or **fe**. If you are unsure, always check in a dictionary and use one of the spelling strategies from Unit 1 to help you remember the correct spelling.

A tip that often works is saying the plural of these words aloud. If you can hear a **v** sound, it usually means the plural ends in **-ves**, for example:

scruffs = **f** sound
calves = **v** sound.

Activity

Read the story below. Change the words in blue into their plural form.

Robin had never seen such a gang of **scruff**, although their clothing blended perfectly with the **leaf** on the bushes and trees all around them. Without exception, they all had long **knife** hanging from their belts and looked very menacing. The men laughed loudly at him, howling like **wolf**. Robin knew he would have to call their **bluff**. "Who are you?" he yelled. "Do you robbers and **thief** have a leader?" Robin gulped as a huge man stepped forward. "I lead these men. They call me Little John." The atmosphere was tense as Robin asked, "I believe this bridge is the only route over the river to Nottingham. Will you let me pass?"

"I don't care what your **belief** are, rich man." He tossed a long, sturdy stick over to Robin. "And now that we both have **staff**, you'll have to beat me if you want to get past."

Although the giant man smiled at him, Robin knew they'd both be fighting for their **life**, with the loser being cast over the **cliff** below them.

Words ending in 'y'

RULES

— If a word ends in a **vowel** before the **y**, just add **s**, for example:

tra**y** → tra**ys**   bo**y** → bo**ys**   donke**y** → donke**ys**

— If a word ends in a **consonant** before the **y**, change the **y** to **i** then add **es**, for example:

count**ry** → count**ries**   ba**by** → ba**bies**   fami**ly** → fami**lies**

Activity 1

The editor of this page does not understand how to turn words ending in **y** into plurals. Read the page carefully and spot all the mistakes. Write out the words correctly.

7.30 PM | **Eastenders**
Three different brewerys are competing to buy the Queen Vic but the bins are full and the emptys are piling up. The chip shop keys go missing. Can copys be cut before the Cornish pastys go off? To add to his worrys, Ian realises his chimneys need rebuilding.

8.00 PM | **Jamie Oliver – The Naked Chef**
Jamie explores a world of unusual currys and chutneys while visiting India. He also displays his versatile qualitys when trying his hand at catering for wedding partys.

9.00 PM | **The Holiday Programme**
From the luxurys found in the world's best hotels to budget getaways. The mysterys of the Norwegian Lakes are experienced on ferrys while the beautys of Madagascar are explored on a range of trekking holidays. Follow the team as they cope with marauding monkeys on safari and all the noveltys of a trip to Disneyland.

10.00 PM | **Match of the Day**
Replays of today's games. Including Goal of the Month and your chance to vote for the worst penaltys ever taken.

11.35 PM | **The 50 funniest ever films**
The result of Tuesday's phone vote. What do the public think are the best comedys ever?

11.45 PM | **Footballing dreams**
The second in this series of documentarys following young teenage footballers hoping to fulfil their dream of playing in the Premier League. The academys of the top clubs really put these young bodys through the ultimate fitness test.

Activity 2

Read the following article. Change the blue words into their plural form.

Doctor Who

Since 1963, Doctor Who has demonstrated uncanny **ability** to banish **bully** from different **galaxy**. His many **enemy** never quite manage to get the better of him. But even though the show is watched in **country** all over the world, success has not come without many **controversy**.

Did you know?

🌍 In the 1970s. moral campaigner Mary Whitehouse complained the **story** were simply too scary.

🌍 **Army** of Daleks and Cybermen meant whole **family** watched Doctor Who from "behind the sofa". This phrase is now commonly used to describe TV shows with frightening content.

🌍 A mother once complained that both her **baby** were terrified by the show's electronic theme music. Doctor Who was the first show to have completely electronic theme music, one of its many **novelty**.

🌍 Shops in **city** around UK reported a drop in trade following an episode that showed window **dummy** coming to life.

Doctor Who still remains a firm date in many **diary**, however, even considering the many **agony** we may suffer from behind the sofa.

Activity 3

With a partner, write down the following words in their plural form.
Then write one paragraph for each group that includes all the words.

1 motorway pony injury jockey

2 valley factory century turkey

3 company allergy policy delay

4 variety strawberry brandy lolly

5 toy birthday delivery emergency

Words ending in 'o'

Activity

Use a dictionary to look up the plural spelling of the following words. With a partner, write sentences that include these plural words.

> piano   mango   igloo   radio   echo   buffalo   hero   Eskimo   kangaroo   tomato
> avocado   studio   mosquito   cello   fiasco   cuckoo   tattoo   banjo

Irregular plurals

Irregular plurals are words that do not need an **-s** to make them plural. There are no rules to help you with irregular plurals. Most of them are very common words, for example:

foot ➜ feet   child ➜ children

 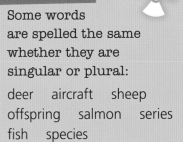
Activity 1

Write down the irregular plural for the following words. You should be able to do most of these without using a dictionary.

> man   mouse   tooth   goose   ox   cactus

Activity 2

Write down the irregular plural for the following words. These are much trickier! Use a dictionary to look up the plural spelling. Write down the meaning of any words you do not understand.

> appendix   curriculum   datum   stimulus   phenomenon
> oasis   larva   criterion   formula   louse

Plurals: self-tests

Complete the tests below. When you have finished, your teacher will have the answers for you to check against.

Self-test 1

Write down the plural form of the words in blue.

1 **Rollerblade** can be dangerous.
2 **Cigarette** can give you lung cancer.
3 Fizzy **drink** can ruin your teeth.
4 We pay too many **tax**.
5 Macbeth met three **witch**.
6 Your **joke** are awful.
7 Look at those lightning **flash**.
8 He always **catch** the ball.
9 A meteorite wiped out all the **dinosaur**.
10 There are more **boss** than workers.

Self-test 2

Write down the plural form of the words in blue.

1 Not all cars have **radio**.
2 He had several **tattoo** on his arms.
3 An orchestra has many **cello**.
4 What are all those **stereo** worth?
5 **Buffalo** have huge, curved horns.
6 Fire all the **torpedo**!
7 Many houses have **patio** nowadays.
8 **Dingo** will eat almost anything.
9 Very few **Eskimo** live in igloos.
10 **Rodeo** are very popular in America.

Self-test 3

Write down the plural form of the words in blue.

1 How many **midwife** do you know?
2 Do all Porsches have **sunroof**?
3 A cat has nine **life**.
4 Road **tariff** are a good idea.
5 **Giraffe** must suffer with sore throats.
6 A good card player can spot **bluff**.
7 A good alarm will deter **thief**.
8 Different tribes have different **chief**.
9 Did all the **dwarf** fancy Snow White?
10 **Sheaf** are gathered at harvest time.

Self-test 4

Write down the plural form of the words in blue.

1 **Motorway** cost a fortune to build.
2 I like westerns where **cowboy** lose!
3 The two **army** faced each other.
4 I hate writing **essay**.
5 **Lorry** should be banned from towns.
6 School **assembly** are so boring.
7 All of the **puppy** survived.
8 Three goals, all from **volley**.
9 Local **community** can be very strange.
10 That field is full of **pony**.

Well done for the answers you got right! If you got any wrong, go back to the part of the unit that will help you and work through the activities again. There are extra activities available to help you.

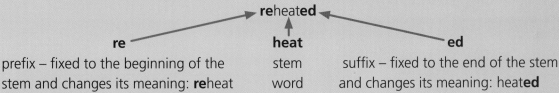

PREFIXES AND SUFFIXES

Many words are made from *prefixes*, *stems* and *suffixes*. For example:

reheat**ed**

re — prefix – fixed to the beginning of the stem and changes its meaning: **re**heat

heat — stem word

ed — suffix – fixed to the end of the stem and changes its meaning: heat**ed**

By the end of this unit you will:
- understand how words are formed
- identify words that contain prefixes, stems and suffixes
- use your knowledge to spell longer words that contain prefixes and suffixes.

Prefixes

RULE

A prefix is a group of letters that are fixed to the **front** of a stem word and change its meaning, for example:

cover
↑
stem

undercover   **re**cover   **un**cover   **dis**cover
↑   ↑   ↑   ↑
prefix   prefix   prefix   prefix

In most cases neither the stem word nor the prefix changes its spelling when they are fixed together.

Activity 1

The main prefixes that you will use are shown below. Use the rule above to match each prefix with a stem word. Write the new words, and label the prefix and the stem.

Prefixes			Stems		
un	anti	im	obey	dress	ground
pre	under	mis	social	build	behave
dis	over	re	even	fix	possible

Activity 2

Write out the words in bold in the paragraph opposite. Underline the **prefix** and circle the **stem**.

I want to **preorder** the new PS3 game. I've played a **preview** on the Internet and it's amazing. I've heard it's **impossible** to complete. I'm **unsure** whether I'll be able to afford it, but my mum says she'll buy me it if I don't **misbehave**. I just hope the game hasn't been **overrated**.

Activity 3

With a partner, make as many words as you can by matching up the prefixes and stems below.

Prefixes		Stems		
mis	im	necessary	spell	numerate
un	under	mature	react	rated
over	il	nerve	solve	rule
dis	in	sent	view	spent	legal

Activity 4

Look at this student's self-assessment. Find the misspelled words and write them out correctly.

I'm good at English but my spelling lets me down. I allmost allways make misstakes with prefixes. It's a big dissappointment when I misspell words like ilegal and imature. The thing is it's unecessary. I just need to get the rule in my head: neither the stem word nor the prefix changes its spelling when they are added together.

Activity 5

Write the answers to these clues. They all contain double letters. You could use a dictionary to help.

Not pleased or contented.	dis _____
Completely unlike.	dis _____
Not essential or required.	un _____
Freaked out.	un _____
Decide against somebody.	over _____
Stops car from moving.	imm _____
Against the laws of nature.	un _____
Spell incorrectly.	mis _____
Young and not fully grown.	im _____
Person who lives forever.	im _____

HANDY HINTS

Do not worry if the last letter of the prefix 'doubles up' with the first letter of the stem. Remember, in most cases neither the prefix nor the stem changes when you fix them together:

dis + similar = di**ss**imilar
un + natural = u**nn**atural

DANGER

'All' is the only prefix that loses a letter when it is fixed to certain stem words, for example:

a**l**though a**l**mighty

Peer-evaluation

Look at the Danger box above. Make a list of the exceptions and make sure you can spell these words correctly. Ask a partner to test you on the spelling of these words

Activity 6

Some of the words in the report below have missing prefixes. Choose the correct prefix for each word from the box and write out the new word. Don't worry if the last letter of the prefix 'doubles up' with the first letter of the stem when you follow the rule, for example: u**n** + **n**atural = u**nn**atural

Prefixes

un   pre   dis   re   under   over   im   mis   il

Teenagers are _____stood to be ___appointed at __official council plans to play classical music at bus stops and other public places to ___courage them from hanging around them at night. __searchers have ___covered that playing the classical tunes causes the children ___comfort. In other words it sends them nuts! One boy __acted with ___belief. "It's __necessary and an ____reaction. People always ___take people my age for criminals. They think we are __mature vandals," he said. Council chiefs __fused to comment.

Peer-evaluation

List all the prefix errors you can find in this passage.

Ugly and unatural scenes at tennis final

The crowd disolved into laughter when disatisfied tennis player Rafael Racket shocked the umpire by climbing into the crowd to assault an unruly fan and leave him imobile on the floor. Later officials declared the commotion unecessary and imoral. They claimed Mr Racket had overreacted and dissqualified him from the competition. They added they were dissappointed that Mr Racket had brought the game into dissrepute.

Swap your work with a partner. Did they identify the same prefix errors? Make a list of any errors they did not spot, then swap back.

Suffixes

RULES

A suffix is a group of letters that are fixed to the **end** of a stem word and change its meaning, for example:

play
↑
stem

playing   **playful**   **played**   **player**
↑   ↑   ↑   ↑
suffix   suffix   suffix   suffix

When a stem ends in a **_consonant_**, in many cases neither the stem word nor the suffix change their spelling when they are fixed together:

colour   colour**ed**   colour**ing**   colour**ful**

Activity 1

Match each stem to the correct suffix below, then write out the new word.

find	**ness**	land	**ship**	joy	**ing**
friend	**est**	sick	**ful**	bright	**ed**

Activity 2

-ing and **-ed** are two of the most commonly used suffixes in English.

1 Using the stem **heat**, write a sentence that includes each of the following suffixes:

   -ed
   -ing

2 Using the stem **view**, write a sentence that includes the following suffixes:

   -ed
   -ing

Activity 3

Write out the words in bold in the diary entry opposite. Underline the **suffix** and circle the **stem**.

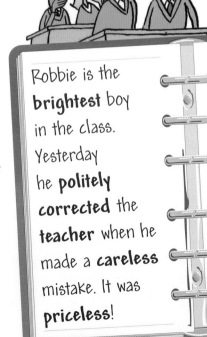

Robbie is the **brightest** boy in the class. Yesterday he **politely** **corrected** the **teacher** when he made a **careless** mistake. It was **priceless**!

The poor old bloke was so angry. The rest of the class just **sniggered** with **amusement**, which further **enraged** him. He **eventually** asked Robbie to get out!

Suffixes: adding -ful to stems

RULE

When the suffix **-ful** is added to a stem word, it only needs one **l**, for example:

care + full = careful

Remember this by thinking: when adding **full** to a stem, be care**ful**!

Activity 1

Look at the holiday brochure below. Find all the words ending in **-ful** and make a note of them.

This beautiful island is a colourful paradise. The delightful blue sea gently laps the wonderful sand and the peaceful villas are right on the beach. The décor in the rooms is tasteful. The service is excellent too. The cheerful staff are helpful and the thoughtful attention to detail makes this a restful holiday. I'd recommend this resort to anyone. You'll be sure to have a successful holiday.

Activity 2

Make a 10 × 10 wordsearch. Squeeze in as many **-ful** words as possible. When you have finished, ask a partner to try to find all your words.

Activity 3

Here are some negative words ending in **-ful**.

awful disgraceful disrespectful dreadful fearful
frightful harmful painful pitiful shameful
stressful tearful ungrateful unsuccessful
untruthful wasteful wrongful distasteful

Imagine you have just visited a terrible holiday resort. Write a letter to the holiday company complaining about it. You could use the model shown opposite as a starting point.

When you have finished your letter, underline the **-ful** words you have used.

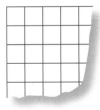

Dear Madam

I write to complain about the disgraceful holiday I have just experienced. There are so many awful things I have to complain about...

Adding suffixes to stems: when to keep the 'e'

RULE

When you add a suffix starting with a **consonant** (**-f**ul, **-m**ent) to a stem ending in **e**, you usually keep the **e**, then add the suffix. For example:

stem	consonant suffix		new word
force	+ ful	=	for**ce**ful
care	+ less	=	car**e**less
state	+ ment	=	stat**e**ment
excite	+ ment	=	excit**e**ment

DANGER

The one exception to this rule is argue + ment which loses the **e** to become **argument**.

Activity 1

Match each stem below with the correct suffix and write down the new word.

hope	move	**ment**	**ful**
price	dark	**ment**	**less**
wire	good	**ness**	**less**
care	advertise	**ness**	**ful**

Activity 2

Study this grid. How many words can you find ending **-ous** or **-able**? Make a list.

A	Z	Y	B	M	X	V	K	X	N	G	L	K
M	D	Q	R	O	O	T	N	R	Y	K	X	P
A	I	V	R	R	F	Q	O	E	X	O	C	L
N	P	O	A	T	U	O	W	C	H	O	O	C
A	O	U	L	N	H	N	L	H	N	E	U	H
G	Y	T	F	Q	T	T	E	A	O	X	R	A
E	W	R	I	M	K	A	D	R	K	I	A	N
A	G	A	K	C	M	N	G	G	W	C	G	G
B	V	G	A	X	E	X	E	E	Z	H	E	E
L	Q	E	I	F	X	A	A	A	O	U	O	A
E	A	O	N	Q	N	V	B	B	H	U	U	B
C	X	U	Y	X	D	J	L	L	S	D	S	L
Z	I	S	Z	N	T	U	E	E	E	O	X	E

HANDY HINTS

1 If a stem ends in **ce** or **ge**, the **e** is kept when the suffixes **able** or **ous** are added:

knowledge**able**
advantage**ous**

2 When a stem ends in **e** and is added to suffixes that start with a vowel (**-able**, **-ing**, **-age**), some words can be spelled with or without an **e**:

stem + suffix	with an 'e'	without an 'e'
like + able	lik**e**able	likable
love + able	lov**e**able	lovable
age + ing	ag**e**ing	aging
mile + age	mil**e**age	milage

When to drop the 'e'

When to drop the 'e'

RULE

When you add a suffix starting with a **vowel** – such as **-able**, **-ed**, **-ing** – (**vowel** suffix) to a stem ending in **e**, you usually drop the **e** before adding the suffix:

describe + ing = *describing*
achieve + able = *achievable*
care + ing = *caring*
excite + ed = *excited*

Activity 1

Join each stem word below to a vowel suffix. Remember to drop the **e** from the stem when you add the suffix.

Stem	Suffix
believe	ation
create	en
disagree	able
educate	er
face	able
force	ing
foresee	ed
love	es

Activity 2

All the stems in the table opposite end in **e**. The suffixes start with either a vowel or a consonant. Copy out and complete the table by adding each stem to the suffix and writing out the new word. Use the rules you have learned to decide whether to keep the **e** on the stem. The first two have been done for you.

Root	+	Suffix	New word
amuse	+	ing	= amusing
care	+	less	= careless
force	+	ful	=
ache	+	ing	=
believe	+	er	=
excite	+	ment	=
spite	+	ful	=
save	+	er	=
forgive	+	ness	=
notice	+	able	=
manage	+	ment	=
home	+	less	=
excite	+	ed	=
recharge	+	able	=
agree	+	ment	=
desire	+	able	=

Peer-evaluation

Swap your table from Activity 2 with a partner. Mark each other's answers. How many did you get right?

43

Suffixes and stems: doubling

RULE

When you add a suffix that starts with a vowel (**-ed**, **-er**, **-ing**) to a stem that ends in a **consonant**, you usually need to double the last letter of the stem. For example:

slip + ed = slipped   *slip + ing = slipping*

slip + er = slipper   *slip + y = slippy ('y' as a vowel sound 'e')*

This rule only applies to words that have:

- ONE syllable: (**slip**)
- ONE short vowel: (sl**i**p)
- ONE consonant as the final letter: (sli**p**)

This is known as the ONE, ONE, ONE rule.

Activity 1

Try the ONE, ONE, ONE rule on the words below. Take the rule step by step.

Step 1
Write out the words from the list below that have **one syllable**.

pat	space	clip	grape	sky
feel	glad	bet	train	throb
pay	bed	trap	workman	red
quit	clap	stem	stab	rid
dragon	sad	fishing	people	star
dream	bar	stop	burst	fail
treat	pet	tree	tap	trek

Step 2
Read through your list of one-syllable words. Underline words with **one short vowel** sound, for example: p**a**t (but not p**ay)**.

Step 3
Look at the underlined words. Tick the words that have **one consonant as the final letter**, for example: ta**p**.

Activity 2

You should now have a list of 18 words that fit the ONE, ONE, ONE rule. Choose ten of these words and match them to the vowel suffixes below. Write out the new word. Remember to double the final consonant of the stem word.

-er	-ish	-ing	-en	-ed

Activity 3

The green words in the article below are missing a vowel suffix. Copy them out and add the correct suffix. Don't forget to use the doubling rule.

-ed	-er	-ing

Skip____ , not a quit____

When Bear Grillpan made his record-breaking walk to the North Pole without any shoes he needed to be fit____ and stronger than the rest. The skip____ was not a quit____! He grab____ the opportunity by the throat, get____ into the record books by swim____ across freezing lakes and dip____ his toes in arctic ice. For food he survived on helicopters drop____ food parcels and trap____ wild creatures with his bare hands. There was no stop____ and sit____ around for Bear Grillpan. Most of the time he was run____ and skip____ ! Trek____ across the frozen wilderness doesn't get any harder than this.

Peer-evaluation

Work with a partner. Take it in turns to identify words in these lists that fit the ONE, ONE, ONE rule.

1	tap	tree	sit	greenhouse	celebrity	quit	ship
2	steel	fit	detail	nap	because	jet	flower
3	drip	sun	sap	dreadful	mop	plop	very
4	pit	whip	pop	wanted	strip	carpet	fever
5	blind	goat	lip	trip	fun	hated	kit
6	worm	rip	shocker	deal	trap	grip	zip

Suffixes and stems: the 'l' rule

RULE

If you add a suffix that starts with a vowel (-**e**d, -**i**ng)
to a stem that ends with an **l**, double the **l**:

marvel ➜ *marve**llou**s*
travel ➜ *trave**lling***

DANGER

Exceptions!
If the **l** follows a pair
of vowels, it is never
doubled, for example:

app**ea**l → appealing
conc**ea**l → concealing

Activity 1

Look at the table below. It shows many common examples
of words that require the **l** to be doubled when a vowel
suffix is added. Some students have tried to complete the
words correctly. How successful have they been?

Stem ending 'l'	+l	vowel suffix	complete word?
cancel	+l	ing	cancelling
cancel	+l	ation	cancellation
control	+l	ing	controling
label	+l	ed	labeled
travel	+l	er	traveller
travel	+l	ed	travelled
quarel	+l	ing	quarelling
panel	+l	ed	panelled
model	+l	ing	modeled

Activity 2

Write out this passage using the **l** rule to complete the words
in purple. Choose from the vowel suffixes in the box below.

| -ous | -ed | -ing | -ers |

THE MARVEL____ MOUNT RUSHMORE MEMORIAL, SOUTH DAKOTA

Between 1927, and 1941, 400 men channel____ their energies into chisel____
these colossal 18 metre high carvings that are model____ on the first six presidents
of America. Workers used dynamite and shovel____ away more than 450,000
tonnes of granite during the project. It is a fact that the compel____ sculptures
were almost cancel____ because of quarrel____ over money. These unrival____
designs attract travel____ and tourists from all over the world. Many thought that
Mr Gutzom Borglum, the chief sculptor, would be propel____ to stardom after his
achievement, but unfortunately he died before the project was finished.

Suffixes and stems: changing 'y' to 'i'

RULES

Here's what to do when adding a suffix to words that end in **y**.

- If there is a **vowel** before the **y**, just add the suffix, for example:

  del**a**y → delayed
  destr**o**y → destroying
  j**o**y → joyful

- If there is a **consonant** before the **y**, change **y** to **i**, then add the suffix, for example:

  var**y** → var**ied**
  occup**y** → occup**ied**
  cit**y** → cit**ies**

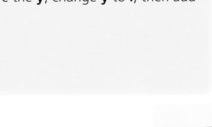

Activity 1

Read the report opposite. Choose a suffix from the box below to add to each blue word. Write out the new words.

ies	iest	ed	ied	ly	ment
ful	fully	ly	er		

Activity 2

Read the review below. Choose suffixes from the box below to complete each blue word, using the rules above. Write out the new words.

ies	ing	ied	iest	ed	ment	ous

The annual Miss Universe contest in Barnsley, England, was won by the **pretty** and most **beauty** contestant, Miss Pluto. She was the **happy** contestant at the show, **envy** by all the others. The **joy** occasion was **easy** the highlight of Miss Pluto's year and was made even better when she immediately announced she was soon to get **marry** to a man from Neptune. "I love this **employ**," she said. "I'm **busy** than ever since I had my plastic surgery. I believe in saving the planets and interplanetary peace," she said **merry**.

When our planet's spaceships are destroy by vicious enemy and terrify aliens using mighty weapons to attack people on Earth, only one person exists with the exceptional quality needed to win...YOU! When victory come thick and fast, injury are ignored and the ability of a Starship Commander are everything, you must save the Earth...

Experience:
* the massive enjoy of 56 multiplayer levels
* the heavy array of weapons known to man.

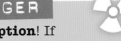

DANGER

Exception! If you add the suffix **-ing** to a word ending in **y**, whether it has a **vowel** or **consonant** before the **y**, always just add **-ing**. For example:

carry → carry**ing**

Prefixes and suffixes: self-tests

Complete the tests below. When you have finished, your teacher will have the answers to check against.

Prefixes: self-test

Choose the correct spelling of the words in blue, below. Write down the correctly spelled word.

1 The paint is **almost/allmost** dry.
2 Boys are **imature/immature** compared to girls.
3 Pupils **missbehave/misbehave** in French lessons.
4 The football referee **overruled/overuled** the linesman.
5 The **inumerable/innumerable** fouls spoiled the match.
6 I totally **disagree/dissagree** with your opinion on that.
7 That footballer is **underated/underrated** in my opinion.
8 He was **dissatisfied/disatisfied** with the final result.
9 "I **dissallowed/disallowed** that man's goal," said the ref.
10 That horror story she told was very **unerving/unnerving**.

Suffixes: self-test

Make two lists of the suffixes in the words below:
a) suffixes that start with a vowel
b) suffixes that start with a consonant.

1 excitement
2 forgiving
3 amusement
4 careless
5 graceful
6 priceless
7 hopeful
8 washable
9 happiness
10 gamesmanship

Suffixes: self-test

Add a suffix to each word in red below, so that each sentence makes sense. Write out the new word.

1 The trick worked **brilliant____** !
2 The **relax____** holiday did us good.
3 He's so **boast____** , I'm sick of it.
4 This **friend____** means an awful lot to me.
5 The local **report____** writes rubbish.
6 That was an **outrage____** foul.
7 That **football____** gets paid far too much.
8 The **Dark____** is a brilliant band.
9 That bed was so **comfort____** .
10 The operation was very **pain____** .

Suffixes: self-test 4 :
Suffixes and stems: 'y' to 'i' rule

Add a suffix to each word in green below, so that each sentence makes sense. Write out the new word.

1 Treasure Island is about **bury____** treasure.
2 That goal has been disallowed. The celebrations will have to be **delay____** .
3 Kitty was well known for her **clumsy____** .
4 **Carry____** heavy weights incorrectly can damage your back.
5 I find boy bands very **annoy____** .
6 I spent all my birthday money and now I'm **penny_** .
7 That joke is the **funny____** I've ever heard.
8 What a **beauty____** car. How much did you pay for it?
9 Some schools have a problem with **bully____** .
10 She's the **brainy____** girl in the class but she's not a genius.

Suffixes: self-test 5 : Suffixes and stems: 'e' rule

Add a suffix to each word in orange below, so that each sentence makes sense. Write out the new word.

1 My dad can't wait for his retire____ .
2 The girl polite____ helped the boy pick up his papers.
3 Sunburn has caused sore____ .
4 Age____ affects people in different ways.
5 You're unbelieve____ !
6 When did you change the arrange____ for the hols?
7 I force____ the back door open.
8 I'm close____ watching the football results.
9 Late____ will lead to detention in this school.
10 Your cruel actions are unforgive____ !

Suffixes: self-test 6 : Suffixes and stems: 'l' rule.

Choose the correct spelling of the words in purple, below. Write down the correctly spelled word.

1 **Cheerfulness/cheerfullness** is a valuable personality trait.
2 **Cancelling/canceling** the holiday will incur charges.
3 Does swearing at a teacher get you **expeled/expelled**?
4 The **traveler/traveller** had never had a proper job.
5 What a **marvellous/marvelous** teacher he is.
6 **Signaling/signalling** failures cause most late trains.
7 The French Revolution was a massive **rebelion/rebellion**.
8 Product **labelling/labeling** now shows how healthy foods are.
9 **Controlling/controling** this remote control plane is difficult.
10 Moles are known for their **tunneling/tunnelling** skills.

Suffixes: self-test 7 : Suffixes and stems: doubling

Choose the correct spelling of the words in blue, below. Write down the correctly spelled word.

1 What a **chaty/chatty** old gossip that woman is.
2 My new brace was **fitted/fited** yesterday.
3 **Stopping/stoping** smoking will improve your health.
4 The weather is **suny/sunny** today.
5 The dog has never been **weter/wetter**.
6 I've been **runing/running** in preparation for the marathon.
7 I've been **treated/treatted** really badly by my best friend.
8 These energy saving bulbs are **dimmer/dimer** than normal ones.
9 The **joger/jogger** is in training for a triathlon.
10 **Hiden/hidden** caves were recently discovered.

WELL DONE for the answers that you got right! If you got any wrong, go back to the part of the unit that will help you. Work through the activities again until you get them right.

COMMON LETTER PATTERNS

OBJECTIVES

Many words have common letter patterns and spelling rules that go with them. By the end of this unit you will be able to:

- know the difference between **soft** and **hard** letter sounds and use the rules that go with them
- know when to use **ci** or **cy**
- spell correctly words that have **ph** in them
- use the **i** before **e** rule
- understand when to use **ch**, **sh** or **tch**
- choose between **ou** or **ow** in a word
- select the right **w** letter pattern
- spell **q** words accurately.

Soft and hard letters

The letters **c** and **g** have different sounds in different words.

The letter **c** has a hard sound in these words:
cow   **c**lock   a**c**tor

The letter **g** has a hard sound in these words:
goal   bu**g**   **g**arlic

The letter **c** has a soft sound in these words:
circle   bi**c**ycle   mi**c**e

The letter **g** has a soft sound in these words:
giraffe   ener**g**y   **g**iant

Activity

1 Read the passage below, looking for words with **c** and **g** in them.

> Certain people argue that spelling is something you can't really learn. You're a good speller or you're not – simple as that. Are they using this idea as an excuse for being a dodgy speller?
>
> In actual fact, spelling is definitely something you can get better at. About 85 per cent of English words follow strict spelling rules. Learn the rules and you will notice a huge improvement in your spelling, just like magic.

2 Copy the table below, and write all the words you found in task 1 under the correct heading.

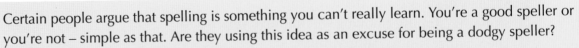

Hard 'c' words	Soft 'c' words	Hard 'g' words	Soft 'g' words

Soft 'c' spellings

RULES

- The letter **c** usually has a soft sound when it is followed by **e**, **i** or **y**, for example:
  *c**e**real   suici**d**e   jui**cy***

- The letter **c** usually has a hard sound when it is followed by **a**, **o**, **u** or a **consonant**, for example:
  *c**a**mera   apric**o**t   c**u**rl   **c**lap*

Activity 1

Read the email opposite. Make two lists:
a) one of hard **c** words
b) one of soft **c** words.

Activity 2

Some people get confused about where they should spell a word with **s** and where they should use a soft **c**. Choose the correct spelling from the pairs below. Use a dictionary if you need help.

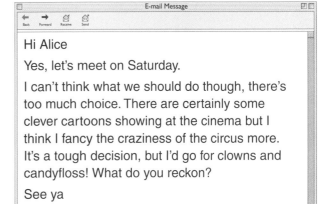

E-mail Message

Hi Alice

Yes, let's meet on Saturday.

I can't think what we should do though, there's too much choice. There are certainly some clever cartoons showing at the cinema but I think I fancy the craziness of the circus more. It's a tough decision, but I'd go for clowns and candyfloss! What do you reckon?

See ya

Lucy :-)

1 fence / fense   2 pierce / pierse   3 vacansy / vacancy
4 cinder / sinder   5 rasism / racism   6 sereal / cereal
7 menase / menace   8 glance / glanse   9 sitizen / citizen

Activity 3

1 Words ending with **-iss** and **-ice** are easily confused. Read these words:

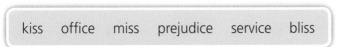

kiss   office   miss   prejudice   service   bliss

2 Count the number of syllables in each of the words above.
   a) How many syllables do the words ending in **-iss** have?
   b) How many syllables do the words ending in **-ice** have?

RULE

Words that rhyme with **-iss** and have more than one syllable are usually spelled **-ice**.
Exception: lettuce!

Activity 4

Words ending with **-ace** can sound very similar to **-iss** / **-ice** endings. Choose the correct spelling from the pairs below. Use a dictionary if you need help. Then write a sentence using the correct spelling of each word.

1 palace / paliss   2 surfice / surface   3 populace / populice
4 grimace / grimice   5 terriss / terrace   6 furniss / furnace

Soft 'cy', 'ce' and 'ci' spellings

RULE

When **c** is followed by **y** or **i** it makes a soft sound, for example:

*cy*mbal *icy* sau*cy* *ci*trus cal*ci*um *ci*nnamon

When **c** is followed by **e** it can also make a soft sound, for example:

*ce*ll *ce*lebrity

Activity 1

Use a dictionary to check the correct spelling for these words. Write a sentence for each one to show you understand its meaning.

1 democracy/sy   2 lunacy/sy   3 ecstacy/sy
4 decency/sy   5 pharmacy/sy   6 prophecy/sy
7 uneacy/sy   8 frequency/sy   9 supremacy/sy
10 clumcy/sy

HANDY HINTS

When you hear a word with a soft sound **-cy**, how do you know when to use **-cy** (as in mer**cy**) or **-sy** (as in mes**sy**)? There are not many rules to help with this, but more words are spelled with the **-cy** ending. Always check in a dictionary if you are unsure.

Activity 2

Read the web page below. The spaces need to be filled. Complete each word correctly using **-cy**, **-ce** or **-ci**.

BREAKING NEWS.

Click a link for more...

- _____anide poison threat in supermarket
  jui_____ for_____s emergen_____ recall.

- _____vil Servi_____ redundan_____ problem

- Divor_____ for _____lebrity chef

- Gla_____ers fa_____ng meltdown crisis

- Defen_____ lawyer blames government complacen_____

Soft 'g' spellings

RULES

- The letter **g** usually has a hard sound when it is followed by **a**, **o**, **u** or a **consonant**, for example:

    gate **g**oal **g**um **g**rim

- The letter **g** usually has a soft sound (like a **j**) when it is followed by **e**, **i** or **y**, for example:

    gentle **g**in**g**er ed**g**y

DANGER

There are quite a few common words where **g** followed by **i** or **e** has a hard sound. Make a note of these words.

get   geese   gear   tiger
gift   girl   give   begin

Activity 1

Sort the following words into those with soft and hard **g** sounds.
Write them out under the correct heading.

> groan gather dog geography sewage bigger digit lounge guilt biology
> goat gum ginger voltage flag gym garden origin gain germ

Activity 2

Read the headlines below. Write out the words in green with the correct spelling for the soft **g** sound.

a _eometry _enius indul_es **his passion for angles**

b _entle _iant **takes the** plun_e

c _ogging bin_es **are bad for your health**

d Young at heart or old for your a_e?

e Shorta_e **of** ma_icians **worries** ma_ic **circle**

f Re_ional **differences in** langua_e **are** hu_e

g Fra_ile _ewel _oins **national museum collection**

'-ge' and '-dge' endings

No English word ends with a **j**. The endings **-ge** or **-dge** are used instead.

- If there is a **consonant** before the soft **g** sound, add **-ge**: *orange*, *diverge*.
- When there is a vowel before the soft **g** sound:
  – if the word is **one syllable** and the vowel is a **short vowel**, the word usually ends in **-dge**:
  *sm**u**dge, dr**e**dge, j**u**dge.*
  – otherwise the word usually ends in **-ge**:
  *mass**a**ge, garb**a**ge, cabb**a**ge.*

Activity

Read the following newspaper article. Write out the words in red with their correct soft **g** ending.

HE_____ DISPUTE CAUSES OUTRA_____

The sleepy village of Holloway erupted with sava_____ scenes of reven_____ earlier this week. An argument concerning a he____ running along the e____ of neighbouring cotta_____s was at the centre of the disturbance. Chris Bigland alle_____s that his neighbour, Lynda Taylor, has carried out a series of attacks on his property. "She claims the he_____ is too high," says Mr Bigland, "But it gives me plenty of privacy. She challen_____d me about it but I told her it was staying. Then stran_____ things began to happen."

Mr Bigland claims that Mrs Taylor has sent foul-smelling packa_____s through the post, one of which contained rotting cabba_____. In addition, thousands of pounds worth of dama_____ was done to his car: "She stuffed sausa_____s up the exhaust pipe and poured porri_____ into the petrol tank. It's completely wrecked; there's no chance of salva_____."

Mrs Taylor was filled with ra_____ when told of the accusations. "Do I look like the sort of person to hold a gru_____ and go on a rampa_____ like that? I acknowle_____ the fact I complained about his he_____ but only because he won't cut it

on my side. I can't mana_____ it at my age. I don't care how tall it is."

With neither side willing to bu_____, the peaceful ima_____ of this beautiful village looks likely to be rava_____d for quite some time.

'ph' words

See Unit 1, page **15** for more on the history of words.

RULE

The **f** sound in a word is usually spelled with **f** or **ff** but it is sometimes spelled with **ph**.

*f*right   tra*ff*ic   dri*f*t   sti*ff*
phoenix   autogra**ph**   ele**ph**ant

Most of the words using the **ph** pattern came from the Ancient Greek language. **Remember:** knowing the origin of words can help you to remember the different spelling patterns.

Activity 1

The incomplete words below all contain the **f** sound. Some are spelled with **ph** and some with **f** or **ff**. Write each word out in full.

1 A micro__one is used for recording sound.

2 The body of a bird is covered in __eathers.

3 Drugs and medicines are bought at a __armacy.

4 A pro__et is someone who predicts the future.

5 A da__odil is a yellow flower.

6 __ysics is a branch of science.

7 A ty__oon is a powerful tropical storm.

8 Per__ume is worn to make you smell nicer.

9 Ty__oid is a deadly disease.

10 Mobile __ones have become much smaller and lighter.

Activity 2

Read the thoughts of the student opposite. Then write each word out in full, using **f**, **ff** or **ph** to complete it.

English lessons used to be ____un but now I've got a real ____obia about them. Learning the al____abet was easy, but since then I've ____elt such a ____ool. Splitting my writing into paragra____s can be a bit tricky although I ____ind that simple compared to some of the other stu____ . Those apostro____es look like ____oating commas to me so getting those right is always a ____luke. I get con____used between meta____ors and similes and eu____emisms scare the living daylights out of me. If it was le____t to me I'd call a hy____en a 'dash', and homo____ones sound like something for sending text messages. It's just not ____air!

'ei' or 'ie' spellings?

RULES

The following rule is useful to remember:

i before **e** except after **c** but only when the **ie** sound rhymes with **me**.

- **i** *before* **e** and rhymes with **me**, for example: *fierce*, *siege*.
- **i** *after* **e** because it doesn't rhyme with **me**, for example: *sleigh*, *eight*.
- **i** *after* **e** when after **c**, for example: *receipt*, *deceive*.

Activity 1

Write out the words in green by completing them with either **ie** or **ei**.

1 Being so close to the **airf__ld** can be very noisy at times.

2 Have you seen that huge crack in the **c__ling**?

3 The leader of the tribe was called **Ch__f** Running Bear.

4 The company had unfortunately gone into **rec__vership**.

5 Would you like another **p__ce** of cake?

6 The Viking carried a large axe and a heavy **sh__ld**.

7 I don't **bel__ve** you ran the 100 metres in nine seconds.

8 There was a **br__f** interval between the two acts of the performance.

9 Lying to me like that was extremely **dec__tful**.

10 The **th__f** pleaded guilty to his crimes.

DANGER

Watch out for the **exceptions** to this rule! Use LOOK, SAY, COVER, WRITE, CHECK to learn them:

seize   protein   weird
caffeine   neither
counterfeit   weir   either
Keith   Neil   Sheila

Activity 2

Read the following letter and choose the right spelling. Write out the correct words.

Dear Laura

I'm sorry to hear you're having so much **grief / greif** with the behaviour of your **niece / neice**. She sounds like a little **fiend / feind**. **Shrieking / shreiking** at the local **priest / preist** like that must have been **unbelievably / unbeleivably** embarrassing. You need all the support you can **recieve / receive** so please don't hesitate to call on me if you need **relief / releif** from the situation.

Your friend,

Elizabeth

DANGER

△ When adding a **suffix** to a word ending in **y**, always use **ie**, even after a **c**, for example: policy → polic**ie**s   fancy → fanc**ie**d

△ **cie words**

When spelling a word where **cie** sounds like **sh**, the **i** comes before the **e**, for example: cons**cie**nce   an**cie**nt   effi**cie**nt   defi**cie**nt   spe**cie**s

△ **Two separate sounds**

If you can hear that an **i** and an **e** make two separate sounds in a word, spell the word as you hear it and ignore the other rules, for example:

client (cl**i** / **e**nt)   obedient (o / be / d**i** / **e**nt)

alien (a / l**i** / **e**n)   glacier (gla / c**i** / **e**r)

Activity 3

Add any suffix to the following words. Look at Units 3 and 4 for extra help.

> reply   agency   currency   tendency   melody
> emergency   injury   frequency   robbery

Activity 4

The **i** and the **e** in the following words make separate sounds. Write each word down, separating the syllables with a line. Notice that the **i** and the **e** are either side of a line. How many syllables are there in each word?

> science   diet   audience   society   convenient
> cashier   experience   premier   variety   ingredient

HANDY HINTS

◆ When the **ie / ei** sound rhymes with **me** it is usually spelled with **ie**, for example: hyg**ie**ne, rel**ie**ve, f**ie**ld.

◆ When the **ie / ei** sound doesn't rhyme with **me** it is usually spelled with **ei**, for example: w**ei**ght, th**ei**r, for**ei**gn.

See Unit 4, page **47** for the rule on suffixes changing from y to i

Peer-evaluation

Write a reply to the letter on page 56. Include as many words as you can with the **ei** and **ie** pattern. Begin your letter like this:

When you have finished, swap your work with a partner. Check that they have correctly used the **ie / ei** letter patterns.

> Dear Elizabeth,
>
> Thank you for your kind letter about my niece. I was grateful to receive it. Since I wrote to you many other things have happened...

'ch' and 'tch' words

Activity 1

Read the following advertisements. Check all the words with **ch** or **tch** patterns in a dictionary and correct the mistakes. Write out the corrected words in full.

New at

Brumby's Butchers – top quality ostrich burgers. *Try them with our special kechup.*

Daly's
dispach riders

– we fetch and carry without a hitch.

Teach yourself artchery from scrach. *No previous experience required.* Apply to Jo Hawkyard at PO Box 235.

Sceetching brakes?
Dodgy cluch?
Engine lost its punch?

Top noch repairs carried out at Belper Autos.

Catch a quick luntch at Marple's Deli. Poatched fish a speciality.

Switch to a brand new kichen with Lilleyman's. Dich the old, bring in the new and watch the value of your home soar.

Mulgrew's single malt Scoch whisky.

Each purtchase with free glass.

Muntch and crunch your way through a delicious packet of Calladine's crisps. There's nothing to mach them.

Private Detective agency. Suspect treatchery? Searching for the truth? All research carried out in strictest confidence. Call Phil Whitney at once.

Activity 2

The words in purple need **ch** or **tch** to complete them. Write out the correct words.

1 The bea___ is scor___ing hot today.

2 Approa___ the area carefully because of the hidden tren___ .

3 Can you rea___ up there and pass me the blea___ ?

4 I drew a chur___ on my ske___ pad.

5 That pi___ is in terrible condition for a Premier League ma___ .

 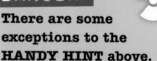

'ch' or 'sh' words

RULE

Many of the words where **ch** sounds like **sh** came into the English language from French, for example:

chateau   chiffon   champagne   Charlotte

Activity

Read the answers to some questions from a quiz. There are some mistakes with the **ch** or **sh** letter pattern. Write out the errors correctly.

'ch' or 'k' words

In some words the letter pattern **ch** has a **k** sound. Most of these words came into the English language from Greek, for example:

tooth**ch**e   **ch**ameleon   an**ch**or
psy**ch**opath   **ch**lorine

Activity

Decide which of the words below is correctly spelled, then write them out.

1 monarch / monark / monarc
2 anarchy / anarky / anarcy
3 napchin / napkin / napcin
4 school / skool / scool
5 choir / koir / coir
6 melancholy / melankoly / melancoly
7 anchle / ankle / ancle
8 chebab / kebab / cebab
9 psychology / psykology / psycology
10 Christmas / Kristmas / Cristmas
11 schedule / skedule / scedule
12 schull / skull / scull
13 technique / teknique / tecnique
14 orchid / orkid / orcid
15 chemical / kemical / cemical

1 Nut with hard white shell and light green flesh.   *pistachio*
2 Looks after sheep.   *shepherd*
3 Drives people around in expensive cars.   *shauffeur*
4 Light fittings made from many pieces of crystal.   *chandelier*
5 A sharp rebound or deflection.   *ricoshet*
6 Hit over the net in badminton.   *chuttlecock*
7 Wear one when jumping from an aircraft!   *parashute*
8 Growth of hair beneath the nose.   *moustashe*
9 Wooden building often used for holidays.   *shalet*
10 Appearing coolly unconcerned or indifferent.   *nonchalant*

See Unit 1, page **15** for the history of words

HANDY HINTS

As there is no rule about when to use **ch** for the sound **k**, you just have to learn the words! Write them in your spelling book.

'ou' letter patterns

RULES

The letter pattern **ou** can make up to eleven different sounds. Here's what to do when spelling words with the sound **ou / ow**.

'ow' is used:

- before the letters **n** or **l** when it is the last letter of a *stem* word such as:

    br**ow**n   gr**ow**l   t**ow**n   sc**ow**l

- at the end of a word or the end of a **syllable** such as:

    c**ow**   h**ow**   fl**ow**er   t**ow**el

'ou' is used:

- for most other words with the sound **ow** such as:

    s**ou**nd   b**ou**nce

DANGER

Watch out for exceptions such as:
crowd   foul   noun

Activity 1

Read the following newspaper article. The words with gaps need **ou** or **ow** to complete them. Write out the correct words in full.

Teenagers banned

Strict measures have been ann____nced that are intended to reduce the number of complaints concerning r____dy incidents in the t____n centre. C____ncil leader Heather Beveridge pron____nced: "We are m____nting this campaign to stop cr____ds of l____ts and yobs hanging ar____nd the shopping precinct and f____ntain in the evenings. I'm dumbf____nded that they're even all____ed ____tside at such a late h____r."

Unsurprisingly local teenagers were not impressed. Matt Boyle, aged 15, argued: "There's never any hassle. We're just hanging ab____t with mates." Suman Sharma, 16, added: "She's just p____er crazy that Beveridge woman, looking for something to p____nce on to grab a few headlines."

Police confirmed that the area did not cause them particular concern. "There's a bit of sh____ting occasionally, but that doesn't am____nt to much," said PC Adam Walton, community officer for the area. "Those kids know the b____ndaries." C____ncillor Beveridge stood her gr____nd, however. "I've received a m____ntain of letters ab____t a c____ntless number of problems. We have the p____wer to impose a ban and that's exactly what we intend to do."

Activity 2

Choose which of the following words are spelled correctly.

1 couch / cowch
2 lounge / lownge
3 surround / surrownd
4 froun / frown

5 voucher / vowcher
6 voul / vowel
7 blouse / blowse
8 proul / prowl

9 mouse / mowse
10 pound / pownd
11 gouge / gowge
12 rebound / rebownd

RULE

The short vowel sound **u** can be spelled using **u** as in:

mug   plug   bucket

It can also be spelled **ou** as in:

touch.

Words ending with the sound **us** are normally spelled **ous** as in:

anxi**ou**s   hide**ou**s   vici**ou**s

However, there are no clear rules to follow. These words have to be learned.

DANGER

Watch out for **ou** words that sound like **oo**, for example:

y**ou**th   c**ou**pon   r**ou**te
c**ou**gar   w**ou**nd (injury)
s**ou**venir

Activity 3

Write down the correctly spelled word from each pair below. Use a dictionary to help you.

1 couple / cuple
2 curious / curius
3 goullible / gullible
4 nourish / nurish
5 nougat / nugat
6 famous / famus

7 odious / odius
8 boutcher / butcher
9 cousin / cusin
10 mouffin / muffin
11 pompous / pompus
12 precious / precius

Peer-evaluation

Read the speech bubble below. The gaps need **ou** or **u** to complete them. Write out the correct words in full. Swap your answers with a partner for checking.

Hi Kelly,
it's me. Did you hear about the
tr_____ble at break today? No? It was
seri_____s, believe me. Two y_____ng kids from Year 7 in
a big argument. Really. Enorm_____s noise they made, you
m_____st have heard it? Think it was to do with a bog_____s
story going around. One was jeal_____s, the other got furi_____s
so the yelling started! There w_____ld have been more tr____ble if
vari_____s teachers hadn't come running. It was obvi_____s
the envi_____s one was to blame, but the other one got
told off too! Honestly! Tell you all about it later.
Bye.

HANDY HINTS

Here's what happens when **r** is added to the **ou** pattern:

or (rhyming with floor):
t**our**, c**our**se, f**our**

our (rhyming with power):
dev**our**, s**our**, h**our**

er (rhyming with her):
lab**our**, hum**our**, j**our**ney

'w' letter patterns

RULE

The letter **w** often changes the sound of a vowel that follows it, for example:

> was   war   worm

When **w** is followed by **a** it sounds like **o** (as in h**o**t), for example:

> want   wallet

Activity 1

Write out the words in blue correctly.

1 My wrist-**wotch** has broken. I **wont** a new one for my birthday.

2 **Whot** was that awful smell that came **wofting** through here?

3 **Wos** it a **wosp** or a bee that stung you?

RULE

When **w** is followed by **ar**, it sounds like **or** (as in f**or**), for example:

> dwarf   wart

Activity 2

The news headlines opposite have some mistakes with the **war** words. How many can you find? Write the headlines correctly.

RULE

When **w** is followed by **or**, it sounds like **er** (as in h**er**), for example:

> worsen, worker

Activity 3

Choose between **er** and **or** to complete the words below. Write down the correct spelling.

1 w___m   **4** w__ld

2 w___thy   **5** w__st

3 w___k   **6** w___ship

DANGER

Watch out for **water** and words that end with silent **e**, such as **wake** and **wave**.

Terrorist wormonger worned by UN

Lukeworm weather causes locust swor

Traffic worden receives safety aword

Students thwort early worning scheme

Move toward postal elections brings no rewords

DANGER

Watch out for **worn**, **worry**, **sword** and words that end with silent **e** such as wo**or**e.

'q' letter patterns

RULE

In English, the letter **q** is always followed by the letter **u**. These two letters are then followed by another **vowel**, for example

squirrel   inquest   quarter

Activity 1

The words in red are all spelled as they sound. They should all contain **qu**. Write out the sentences spelling the words correctly.

1 The moskito bite made me feel kweasy.

2 The peach likewer did not kwench my thirst.

3 Did you akwire tickets for the bankwit?

4 The speaker was elokwent but kwickly put me to sleep.

5 That turkwoise dress is exkwisite.

Activity 2

Write out the correct answers to these questions. Use a dictionary to help you.

1 You do this if you multiply something by four.   qua_____

2 You are 'in' this if you are kept away from everyone else. qua_____

3 To spend wastefully or extravagantly.   squa_____

4 Dirty, run-down and repulsive.   squa_____

5 To get to the next stage of a competition.   qua_____

HANDY HINT

As a rough guide, in a **qua** letter pattern, **qu** sounds like **kw** and **a** sounds like **o**, for example:
s**qu**adron
s**qu**abble
When the letter pattern **que** appears at the end of a word it makes a **k** sound. Most words with this pattern came into English from the French language.

Activity 3

The following words need either **que** or **k** to complete them. Write out the correct words.

A frea____ event occurred during a visit to a local mos____ yesterday afternoon. Visiting mon____s had travelled from Tibet to admire anti____ paintings and other uni____ works of art, when a golden pla____ fell from a wall, striking one of the visitors on the head. Luckily the injury was not serious, although a mar____ was left on the fallen object.

Common letter patterns: self-test

Complete the tests below. When you have finished, your teacher will have the answers to check against.

Self-test 1 : soft 'c'

Write down the words in blue that are spelled correctly.

1 I have a **tendency / tendensy** to ignore **advice / advise**.
2 I have been given **notice / notise** to quit my **tenancy / tenansy**.
3 Walking through wet **cement / sement** was **clumcy / clumsy** of me.
4 You must spell with **precice / precise accuracy / accurasy**.
5 **Cruice / cruise** liners are safe from **piracy / pirasy**.
6 The **agency / agensy** was in the **centre / sentre** of town.
7 Let's **celebrate / selebrate** a **sucsessful / successful** result.
8 The fire was **certainly / sertainly** a case of **arcon / arson**.
9 The **cygnets / sygnets** were sitting beneath the **cedar / sedar** tree.
10 **cycling / sycling** through the **city / sity** saves time.

Self-test 2 : soft 'g'

Write down the words in purple that are spelled correctly.

1 Your **gems / jems** and **gewels / jewels** make me **gealous / jealous**.
2 I **managed / manajed** to eat the **cabbage / cabbaje**.
3 I left my **baggage / baggaje** in the train **carriage / carriaje**.
4 The **general / jeneral** feeling is we must give an **apology / apolojy**.
5 The **gury / jury** listened to the statement from the **hostage / hostaje**.

Self-test 3 : 'ge' or 'dge' endings

Write down the words in green that are spelled correctly.

1 I **trudged / truged** through the snow with my **sledge / slege**.
2 The monkey sat on a **ledge / lege** at the back of the **cadge / cage**.
3 I don't have the **couradge / courage** to make my own **fudge / fuge**.
4 There's no **chardge / charge** for crossing the **bridge / brige**.
5 The **garadge / garage** will replace the **badge / bage** on your car.

Self-test 4 : 'ph'

Write down the correctly spelled words.

1 pamphlet / pamflet
2 phoreign / foreign
3 phrase / frase
4 phantom / fantom
5 cellophane / cellofane
6 phury / fury
7 triumph / triumf
8 pheasant / feasant
9 nephew / nefew
10 orphan / orfan

Self-test 5 : 'ei' or 'ie'

Write down the correctly spelled words.

1 field / feild
2 conciet / conceit
3 brazier / brazeir
4 yield / yeild
5 retrieve / retreive
6 sufficient / sufficeint
7 grieve / greive
8 gradient / gradeint
9 percieve / perceive
10 belief / beleif

Self-test 6 : 'ch' and 'tch'

Write down the correctly spelled words.
1 bloch / blotch
2 scrach / scratch
3 bench / bentch
4 porch / portch
5 drench / drentch
6 staunch / stauntch
7 huch / hutch
8 coach / coatch
9 cruch / crutch
10 wreched / wretched

Self-test 9 : 'ou' / 'u'

Write down the correctly spelled words.
1 courier / curier
2 cactous / cactus
3 glorious / glorius
4 devious / devius
5 trouble / truble
6 blount / blunt
7 loump / lump
8 nervous / nervus
9 double / dubble
10 joyous / joyus

Self-test 7 : 'sh' or 'ch' and 'k' or 'ch'

Write down the correctly spelled words.
1 machine / mashine
2 sachet / sashet
3 chovel / shovel
4 charade / sharade
5 chord / kord
6 chrysalis / krysalis
7 chaos / kaos
8 chayak / kayak
9 chemist / kemist
10 chronic / kronic

Self-test 10: 'w' letter patterns

Decide on the correct vowel for the gaps, then write out the complete word.
1 The sw__n sw__m tow__rd the river bank.
2 You should have forew__rned me about the sw__mp.
3 You need a w__sh; you smell like a w__rthog!
4 You must w__rk your way upw__rds from the bottom.
5 The smell of w__rm w__ffles drifted past them.

Self-test 8 : 'ou' / 'ow'

Write down the correctly spelled words.
1 pouch / powch
2 found / fownd
3 brouse / browse
4 pout / powt
5 bound / bownd
6 allouance / allowance
7 counsel / cownsel
8 counter / cownter
9 gouge / gowge
10 froun / frown

Self-test 11: 'q' letter patterns

Write down the correctly spelled words.
1 square / skware
2 equal / ekwal
3 teaque / teak
4 acquaintance / acwaintance
5 squid / skwid
6 quote / kwote
7 require / rekwire
8 adequate / adekwate
9 beaque / beak
10 request / rekwest

Well done for the answers you got right! If you got any wrong, go back to the part of the unit that will help you and work through the activities again. Your teacher also has additional activities to help you.

COMMON ENDINGS

Common letter patterns occur at the end of many words.
This unit will help you to:

- recognise and improve your spelling of common letter patterns at the end of words
- improve your spelling of endings that sound the same but are spelled differently.

'-ough', '-ought' and '-aught' endings *IWB*

The letter pattern ending **-ough** has a number of different sounds.

Activity 1

Copy out the table opposite. Then read sentences 1–5, looking for the **-ough** words. Write them in the correct place in your table, according to how they sound.

Rhymes with:	stuff	show	scoff	now
	to**ugh**	th**ough**	c**ough**	pl**ough**

1 Pizza dough is really easy to make.

2 The main branch of a tree is called a bough.

3 Last night's ferry crossing was really rough.

4 Although I'm 18 I still can't drive.

5 The cows drank from the trough.

6 He barely had enough money for the bus.

Activity 2

Write your own sentence for each of the following words:

tough   cough   though   plough

The letter pattern endings **-ought** and **-aught** can be said in different ways.

Activity 3

With a partner, complete the words with gaps. All the answers contain either **-ough**, **-aught** or **-ought** letter patterns.

1 My mum b____ me a gift. I never t____ it would be an iPhone.

2 I o____ to tell my dad I got n____ in my maths exam.

3 Boxers are t____ to be t____ !

Peer-evaluation

Draw a 10 cm square grid. Design a word search that includes as many **-ough**, **-ought** and **-aught** words as possible.

Swap grids with a partner. Look for all the **-ough**, **-ought** and **-aught** words in their grid. Then check with them to see if you found them all.

'-ous', '-ious' and '-eous' endings

The **uss** sound at the end of many words can be spelled in three ways: **-ous**, **-ious** and **-eous**. If you listen to the word you are trying to spell, you should be able to choose the correct ending.

'-ous' endings

RULE

The ending **-ous** is the most common letter pattern at the end of an *adjective*, or describing word:

noun		adjective
mountain	➜	mountain**ous**
villain	➜	villain**ous**

Activity 1

Read the news report below. Write out the words that have the **-ous** endings and underline the end pattern.

Dangerous Dave:
fabulous human cannonball

When Dangerous Dave, the famous circus clown, was fired from an enormous cannon, the joyous crowd were understandably nervous! The marvellous man received generous applause as he sailed out of the arena and landed in a monstrous pit of poisonous, venomous snakes. Other performers will only be jealous of his daring stunt. Will this ridiculous bravery ever be repeated?

Activity 2

Write a news report about an attraction or event – for example, you might choose a visit to a theme park or watching a football match. Try to include as many **-ous** words as you can. Underline the words with **-ous** endings. You can use the word bank opposite to help you.

anonymous	luminous
dangerous	marvellous
enormous	monstrous
fabulous	murderous
famous	nervous
generous	poisonous
grievous	raucous
jealous	torturous
joyous	venomous

'-ious' ending

RULES

The ending **-ious** is mainly used in two cases.

1 When you hear the sound **shus** at the end of a word, following the letters **t**, **c** or **x**, for example:

cautious   *vicious*   *anxious*

> **See Unit 5, page 50 for more on soft and hard letters**

2 When you can hear the **i** as a syllable on its own, for example:

hilarious	*hilar / i / ous*
serious	*ser / i / ous*
ingenious	*ingen / i / ous*

Activity 3

Read this text from a website. List the words that end in **-ious**.

Grave robbers hunt precious hidden treasure

From ancient times devious criminals have hunted mysterious treasures hidden in graves! It was a serious business because glorious jewels, money and artefacts were often buried with their owners in the belief that they would come in useful in the afterlife. Ambitious thieves braved infectious diseases and terrible curses to steal them. Many of the most famous cases of grave robbing relate to ancient Egypt, where tombs were often protected by ingenious traps and hidden dangers.

Activity 4

Copy and complete this table. Use words from your list from Activity 3.

'shus' sound following 't', 'c 'or 'x'	'i' as a syllable heard on its own
anxious	mysterious

'-eous' ending

RULE

Use the **-eous** ending when:

- a stem ends in soft **ge**: *outrage* ➔ *outrageous*
- you can hear an **e** in a word as a syllable on its own: *hideous*.

Activity 5

Look at the letter opposite. Write out the words missing **-eous**.

My wife is gorg____ but she wears outrag____ clothes. She thinks she's being courag____ and spontan____ but everyone looks at her like she's crazy. I should tell her about how awful that banana yellow mini-skirt looks but I'm too court____ . She even makes the dog look hid____ !

'-tion', '-ssion', '-cian' and '-sion' endings

'-tion' endings

The **-shun** sound at the end of some words can be spelled in the following ways:

-tion	attention	**-ssion**	session
-cian	politician	**-sion**	division

There are rules that will help you decide which ending to use. They help you to listen to a word carefully and make the right choice.

Activity

Read the advertisement below. Write down the words ending in **-tion**.

- Use the ending **-tion** if you can hear a *long vowel* before the **shun** sound, for example:

    nation   excretion
    emotion   evolution

- Use the ending **-tion** if there is a *consonant* before the **shun** sound, for example:

    section   addiction

- Use the ending **-tion** after a *short vowel* **i** sound when the word doesn't end in **-mission**, for example:

    tradition   competition

PETE'S PUMP-ACTION PAINTBALL PARK

Forget relaxation and get in on the action. Join the paintball sensation! Enjoy the exhilaration of battle and use our new powerful paintball weapons of mass destruction! Make a bid for world domination. Finish off the competition and paint the opposition!

In addition, why not take advantage of our two for one promotion? Plus:
* free accommodation   * free weapon instruction
* free tuition solutions

Join the revolution at Pete's Paintball Park.

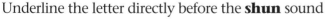

Activity

Underline the letter directly before the **shun** sound in each word that you wrote down in Activity 1. Make a table like the one opposite. Sort the words you have found into the correct columns.

'-tion' (long vowel before 'shun' sound)	'-tion' (consonant before 'shun' sound)	'-tion' (after short vowel 'i' sound doesn't end -mission)
sensation	instruction	tuition

'-ssion' endings

- Use the ending **-ssion** if you can hear the **short vowel** sounds **a**, **e** or **u**, before the **shun** sound, for example:

  passion   *aggression*   *discussion*

- Use the ending **-ssion** after the short vowel **i** when the word ends with **-mission**. Otherwise use **-ition**.

short 'i' ending '-mission'	short 'i' not ending '-mission'
permission	*tradition*
admission	*audition*

Activity 3

Read the following TV listings. Write out the words that have the **-ssion** letter pattern, and underline the short vowel that comes before it.

7.30pm   *The Z Factor*
Watch wanabees who have an obsession with entering the celebrity profession.
These crooners want to make an impression on the judges. Half the fun is the discussion between the panel, because Simon Towel is always full of aggression while Cheryl Troll always shows compassion. Every contestant is seeking admission to the next round, to avoid the depression of failure. The best bit is the tension when they wait for the judges' permission to go through. It's rubbish, but I must make a confession…I watch it every week.

Activity 4

Test your understanding of words ending in **-ssion** or **-tion**. The words below need to be completed with either **-ssion** or **-tion**. Write down the correct words.

1 opposi_____	5 ambi_____	9 competi_____	13 condi_____
2 tradi_____	6 percu_____	10 obse_____	14 relaxa_____
3 proce_____	7 discu_____	11 consola_____	15 submi_____
4 defini_____	8 compa_____	12 permi_____	16 destruc_____

'-cian' endings

Activity 5

Read the rule box opposite. With a partner, think of four other jobs with the **-cian** ending.

'-sion' endings

Activity 6

Use the **-sion** ending to write down the whole words begun in blue.

1 The **ten____** towards the end of the match was unbearable.

2 My granddad is 65, so now he's started to collect his **pen____** .

3 A mirage is an **illu____** in the desert.

4 Getting a person to do something is called the art of **persua____** .

5 My holiday was a brilliant **occa____** .

6 There's never anything on **televi____** .

7 When I make a **deci____** I stick to it.

Activity 7

Read the report below. The words in red need to be completed with one of these endings: **-tion**, **-cian**, **-ssion** or **-sion**. Write down the correct words. Use a dictionary if you need help.

Most people love watching fast-action anima_____ films like *Shrek* or *Wallace and Grommit* at the cinema or on televi_____ . But did you know that these days anima_____ is within reach of anyone with a computer, decent software and the ambi_____ ? If you have the vi_____ and the pa_____ , you can create wonderful stop-mo_____ films and become a techni_____ of the artform. The deci_____ is yours to create a perfect expre_____ of your imagination. You decide the loca_____ , the story, the conclu_____ . Whatever your inten_____ , give it a try!

'-le', '-el' and '-al' endings

'-le' endings

Most words ending in the **-ul** sound are spelled with **-le** such as batt**le**. There are no clear rules, but the activities below will help you.

Activity 1

Find the 13 words ending **-le** in this wordsearch. Write them out.

'-el' endings

E	D	B	U	B	B	L	E	S	H
J	F	D	E	N	A	B	L	E	N
F	A	B	L	E	M	J	Q	H	Q
C	H	M	I	Z	T	A	B	L	E
B	A	D	O	U	B	L	E	D	P
Q	O	C	I	R	C	L	E	A	L
V	Z	T	K	L	I	G	B	Z	U
O	D	P	T	L	T	F	Q	Z	F
W	E	A	G	L	E	C	L	L	M
B	U	C	K	L	E	Y	O	E	S

RULE

The **-el** ending is commonly used after the following letters:

n: chan**nel**
r: bar**rel**
s: wea**sel**
v: re**vel**
w: to**wel**
soft c: par**cel**
soft g: an**gel**

Activity 2

The table below shows examples of the -el ending, after the letters n, r, s, v, w, soft c and soft g. Choose one word from each column of this table. Invent one sentence for each word.

channel	quarrel	easel	level	trowel	angel
flannel	barrel	diesel	shovel	towel	bagel
panel	cockerel	chisel	travel	vowel	cancel
kennel	squirrel	tinsel	novel	jewel	parcel
tunnel	scoundrel	vessel	marvel	bowel	excel

Activity 3

Test your partner. Can they remember the letters below to help them with **el** word endings?

N   R   S   V   W   C   G

'-al' endings

- **-al** is often used as an ending for an ***adjective*** (describing word), for example: magic**al** spell. Here the **-al** makes the word mean 'to do with': to do with a spell
- A few words ending in **-al** are nouns or naming words. There is no rule to tell you whether to use **-al**, for example:
  decim**al**   med**al**
  cathedr**al**   materi**al**

Activity

Read the advert below, which shows a number of adjectives with the **-al** ending. Write out the words and underline the **-al** ending.

Paranormal Investigations Agency

Some folks are sceptical about the supernatural, but if you are plagued by magical and mystical events in your house, you know these events can be a real trial.

- *Are you going mental because ancestral spirits, ghosts, phantoms and brutal banshees are causing havoc in your house?*
- *Are you fed up with historical figures visiting you in the middle of the night?*

We will ensure your survival by banishing unconventional and unusual ghouls with our special techniques. Total peace of mind; exceptional results guaranteed. Don't get hysterical, get even! Put your home back to normal now! Full national service call 0900 00000.

Activity

Use your imagination. Create an advert of your choice using as many **-al** words as possible. Use the word bank below to help.

abnormal	classical	digital	experimental
accidental	colossal	disposal	fatal
alphabetical	conventional	educational	historical
archaeological	cosmological	electrical	identical
artificial	critical	equal	international

Peer-evaluation

Swap your advert from Activity 2 with a partner. Can they find and underline every word ending **-al**? Who used the most **-al** words?

'-able' and '-ible' endings

There is no clear rule to help you choose when to use the ending **-able** (as in un**able**) or **-ible** (as in ined**ible**), but two things may help you.

1 More words end in **-able** than **-ible**.

2 You can sometimes hear whether the ending is **-able** or **-ible**, for example: sens**ible** or break**able**.

'-able' endings

Activity 1

Read the problem page below. Find all the words that end in **-able** and write them out.

Your problems ...

Dear Bunty

My daughter used to be so dependable but now she has become so unreasonable. She seems to think it's fashionable to go out with a really unsuitable boy. He has long greasy hair, several rings through his nose and he smells. He's so miserable and he speaks in words of one syllable. A yeti would be preferable!

I can't help feeling this is all avoidable. I need help fast. Why can't I have my nice reasonable and predictable daughter back?

Activity 2

Here are some more words with the **-able** ending. Write a sentence for each.

irritable
available
agreeable
desirable

'-ible' endings

Activity 3

Look at these pairs of spellings. Choose the correct ending. Then, for each word, write a sentence.

1 sensible / sensable

2 incredible / incredable

3 audible / audable

4 impossible / impossable

5 accessible /accessable

6 horrible / horrable

7 invisible / invisable

'-ical', '-icle' and '-acle' endings

'-ical' endings

The **-ical** ending is often used at the end of an adjective, or describing word. Further examples of the **-ical** ending are:

myst**ical**   opt**ical**   chem**ical**   econom**ical**

Activity 1

Many **-ical** adjectives are used in your school subjects. Make a table like the one below. Complete the missing letters. They are arranged according to subject areas.

Science and Technology	Arts and Humanities
m_dical	_lphabetical
lo_ical	ly_ical
biolo_ical	m_taph_rical
o_tical	m_sical
pra_tical	h_st_rical
tec_nical	g_ographical
_echanical	ph_sical
el_ctrical	bi_lical
che_ical	p_litical
cli_ical	cr_tical
a_trono_ical	clas_ical

Activity 2

Work in pairs. Pick a column of words from the table in Activity 1 and test each other. Use the LOOK, COVER, SAY, WRITE, CHECK steps to learn any words you spell incorrectly.

Activity 3

Write out these headlines. Underline the ending pattern **-ical**.

Critical chemical leak at electrical factory

Medical miracle in optical hospital

Classical musical flops

Political scandal hits government

Fake painting identical to original

Mechanical fault causes technical failure

'-icle' and '-acle' endings

Activity 4

Look at these film titles. Find the words containing **-icle** or **-acle**. Write them in two separate columns according to their ending.

Kraken: Tentacles of the Deep (1996)
Barnacle Bill (1957)
Nancy Drew: The White Wolf of Icicle Creek (1997)
Miracle on 34th Street (1947)
The Oracle (1985)

Particles in Space (1966)
Chronicles of Narnia (2005)
Article 99 (1992)
Obstacle (2005)

Activity 5

Read this review of one of the films above. Find all the words ending **-icle** or **-acle** and add them to your list.

Blistering barnacles: what a spectacle!

When Dan Deep dives down to chronicle an old shipwreck we can guess he's heading for disaster! In his submarine vehicle he encounters all manner of obstacles…not least a 50ft tentacle. Yes you've guessed it! A mammoth squid likes crushing humans for fun. It grabs him in a manacle like grip and won't let go. This is the pinnacle of Hollywood entertainment and what a surprise… by some miracle Dan Deep survives. Hooray!

Activity 6

Write an imaginary review of another film title from above. Include as many **-icle** and **-acle** words as you can!

Activity 7

Read this report. Several words are wrong. Find them, then write them out with the correct spelling.

According to a recent artical a new miricle cure for baldness has just been announced by medicle experts. It's a chemicle that has been proved in clinacle trials. Patients were criticle at first but now say it works. Doctors say it is effective because it strengthens every individual hair follical.

'-ence' and '-ance' endings

Activity 1

Use the word bank below to work out the answers to the clues that follow. Remember to write the correct ending for each word!

HANDY HINTS

The word endings **-ance** (as in gl**ance**) and **-ence** (as in indiffer**ence**) sound very alike. There are no rules to help you decide which ending to use.

Words ending '-ance	Words ending '-ence'
adv**ance**	differ**ence**
dist**ance**	excell**ence**
entr**ance**	exist**ence**
fin**ance**	sent**ence**
rom**ance**	def**ence**

1 A group of words that start with a capital letter and end with a full stop.

2 To move forward.

3 The quality of being outstanding or superior.

4 The space separating two things.

5 A novel or film with love as its theme.

6 Another word for money.

7 A door or gate that people enter through.

Activity 2

Find the **-ence** and **-ance** words in this extract. List them in two columns according to which ending they have.

In old England, castles were used for defence. Violence was common, and kings and princes needed a safe residence. A well-protected stronghold would ensure dominance over rivals. Sometimes an enemy did advance. They were denied admittance at the entrance by a strong portcullis. Other measures were more deadly still. Boiling oil was used for instance, being poured from the battlements onto invaders.

Activity 3

With a partner, find the **-ance** and **-ence** mistakes in this piece. If you find nine errors, then well done. You have mastered **-ance** and **-ence** endings!

When 'Evil the Weavel' ace stunt motorbike rider tried to jump a new record-breaking distence last week, he ended up in an ambulence. He tried to make a clearence of 52 double-decker buses but his unsuccessful performence shocked the audiance. There's no doubt about his usual competance on the bike: he's got so much experiance, but in this instence he lost his balence and slam dunked!

'-ate' and '-ite' endings

The endings **-ate** (as in calcul**ate**) and **-ite** (as in appet**ite**) are usually quite easy to tell apart.

- The ending **-ate** is used most often, and the long vowel sound 'a' can be heard very clearly: anim**ate**

- The ending **-ite** usually sounds like a long vowel sound 'i': exc**ite**

- In some words the ending **-ite** sounds like a short vowel sound 'i': favour**ite**, oppos**ite**, gran**ite**

Activity 1

Write down the answers to the clues below. Use a thesaurus if you need help. Each answer ends in **-ate**. The first letter of each answer will reveal a secret message when read in order.

1 Straight away.   ___ediate

2 Work as a team.   ___perate

3 Determined not to agree with others.   ___tinate

4 To find the best route to somewhere.   ___igate

5 To produce energy.   ___erate

6 To do up a property.   ___ovate

7 To speed up.   ___elerate

8 To put up with something.   ___erate

9 The very best.   ___imate

10 To oil moving parts.   ___ricate

11 To enjoy.   ___reciate

12 Put into another language.   ___nslate

13 An approximate calculation.   ___imate

14 Unlucky.   ___ortunate

The secret message is _ / _ _ _ _ _ _ _ _ _ _ _ _ / _

Activity 2

Find the **-ite** words in these songs and write them out in a table like the one below. Identify whether the **-ite** sounds like a short vowel **i** or a long vowel **i**.

'-ite' sounding like a short vowel 'i'	'-ite' sounding like a long vowel 'i'
favourite	dynamite

'I Feel Like Dynamite' (1976)
'My Favourite Things' (1993)
'Write the Songs' (2000)
'White Christmas' (1942)

'Reet Petite (The Finest Girl You Ever Want to Meet)' (1957)
'Satellite of Love' (1972)
'Shoplifters of the World Unite' (1987)

Activity 3

With a partner collect other examples of words ending **-ite**. Write these into the table you started in Activity 2 according to their sound.

Common endings: self-tests

Complete the tests below. When you have finished, your teacher will have the answers to check against.

Self-test '-ous', '-ious' or '-eous'

Each word beginning below ends in **-ous**, **-ious** or **–eous**, and means the same as the definition in brackets. Write out each word correctly.

1 ted   (boring and mundane)
2 gorg   (beautiful, very attractive)
3 court   (polite and considerate)
4 danger   (risky)
5 ingen   (clever and original)
6 prec   (highly valued)
7 cur   (eager to know)
8 courag   (brave in danger)
9 fam   (celebrity)
10 delic   (beautiful taste)
11 poison   (harmful chemical)
12 hid   (awful, disgusting)
13 scrumpt   (very pleasing, tasty)
14 obv   (very clear)

Self-test 2 '-tion' and '-ssion'

Each word beginning below ends in ends in **-tion** or **-ssion** and means the same as the definition in brackets. Write out each word correctly.

1 po   (magical mixture)
2 adora   (great love and esteem)
3 posse   (owning or holding something)
4 aggre   (threatening actions)
5 comple   (finishing something)
6 mo   (movement)
7 instruc (what must be done)
8 emo   (feelings)
9 exhibi   (a public display)
10 emis   (from a factory chimney)

Self-test 3 '-cian' and '-sion'

Each incomplete word below ends in **-cian** or **-sion**. Write out each word correctly.

1 The worst thing about exams is the revi____ .
2 The beauti____ made an ugly woman beautiful.
3 The best penalty kicks are taken with preci____ .
4 Coastal ero____ is a serious problem on the East coast.
5 The mathemati____ solved a difficult equation.
6 The explo____ brought the derelict building down.
7 I watch televi____ for about six hours each day.
8 The electri____ has rewired our house.
9 I live in a man____ with 15 rooms.
10 An opti____ tests people's eyesight.

Self-test 4 '-le', '-el' and '-al'

Each word below ends in **-le** or **-el**. Write out each word correctly.

1 bang__
2 unc__
3 beet__
4 jew__
5 bott__
6 lab__
7 rust__
8 cack__
9 dazz__
10 tow__

Each word below ends in **-le** or **-al**. Write out each word correctly.

1 dood__
2 met__
3 fizz__
4 roy__
5 fin__
6 gamb__
7 gigg__
8 actu__
9 glob__
10 norm__

Self-test 5 '-ical', '-icle' and '-acle'

Each word started below ends in **-ical**, **icle** or **-acle** and is the answer to the clue in brackets. Write out each word correctly.

1 ic____   (spike of frozen water)
2 geograph____ (matters to do with the world)
3 com____   (highly amusing)
4 bibl____   (concerning the bible)
5 med____   (concerning medicine)
6 chron____   (historical document)
7 log____   (clear and reasonable)
8 part____   (tiny speck of matter)
9 tent____   (part of an octopus)
10 cub____   (small changing room)

Self-test 6 '-ance' and '-ence'

Each word below ends in **-ance** or **-ence**. Write down the word correctly.

1 intellig____
2 sil____
3 evid____
4 sent____
5 appear____

Self-test 7 '-ate' and '-ite'

Each word below ends in **-ate** or **-ite**. Write down the word correctly.

1 indefin__
2 inv__
3 favour__
4 oppos__
5 defin__

Well done for the answers you got right! If you got any wrong, go back to the part of the unit that will help you and work through the activities again. Your teacher also has additional activities to help you.

SPELLING AND PUNCTUATION

OBJECTIVES

**This unit will help you to spell correctly words that involve punctuation.
By the end of this unit you will be able to:**

- correctly use capital letters
- correctly use apostrophes
- correctly understand that apostrophes are used in two different ways
- correctly use hyphens
- know when to use one word or two.

Capital letters

The rules for using capital letters are quite simple,
but people are often careless when using them!

Activity 1

RULES

Use capital letters for:

- the beginning of a sentence (***W****ith hard work your spelling will improve.*)
- all proper nouns (***W****ales,* ***J****ames,* ***E****astenders,* ***N****ike*)
- words that are derived from proper nouns (***W****elsh,* ***S****cottish,* ***L****iverpudlian*)
- the pronoun **I** or any abbreviations involving **I** (***I****'ve,* ***I****'m,* ***I****'ll*)
- the first word of speech (*Carolynn said, "****C****an we play table-tennis?"*)
- initials (***FBI   GB   BBC***)
- days of the week and months of the year (***T****uesday,* ***J****anuary*)
- names of specific events (***G****lastonbury* ***F****estival,* ***D****iwali*)
- titles (***Mr   Mrs   Dr***)

The following sentences have no capital letters.
Write them out again, putting in the capital letters.

> **1** when stoke city play notts county on sunday, the two oldest football teams in the globe are facing each other.
>
> **2** the man said "do you know what tom? i'm really proud to be a londoner and i can't wait for the olympic games to start here."
>
> **3** even though shaakirah loved pepsi, she had a soft spot for dr pepper too.
>
> **4** adam asked "are you watching coronation street on tv tonight?" sam replied, "no, i'm going into manchester to see my uncle eric."

Activity 2

This magazine article has no capital letters.
Write it out again, putting in the capital letters.

> *star wars* is probably the most successful film franchise of all time. the first film, *episode IV: a new hope*, was released in 1977. since then, a further six films have been released, earning approximately $2.5 billion in the usa alone. characters such as darth vader and yoda are recognised around the entire world and the cultural impact of the films is huge. 390,000 english fans even named the jedi "faith" as their official religion, according to a census taken in 2001.
>
> when the actor alec guinness said "may the force be with you", little did he know that, years later, this short line would become the source of the religion's "official" day of celebration. "may the force" sounds very similar to "may the 4th", and so this day was adopted by fans. don't be surprised to hear the following conversation in early summer:
> "happy star wars day!"
> "what?"
> "may the 4th be with you!"

DANGER

Never use capital letters where they are not needed. In an examination you will lose marks if you:
△ use a capital letter in the middle of a word
△ use 'large' letters at the beginning of a word where a capital is not needed.
If your writing includes either of the above, change your style! Claiming "It's just the way I write" will not help you.

ascender

Size matters. Stop your bad habits now. ← page line

descender

Activity 3

Write around 100 words about your first day at school, or your favourite hobby or your proudest achievement. DO NOT include any capital letters.

When you have finished, swap your work with a partner and correct their work.

Swap back to see if all your deliberate mistakes were spotted.

Apostrophes of abbreviation

The apostrophe of abbreviation shows where a letter or letters have been missed out of a word:

I will	you have	we are	we shall	let us	have not
↓	↓	↓	↓	↓	↓
I'll	you've	we're	we'll	let's	haven't

HANDY HINTS

Apostrophes have two uses:

◆ to show abbreviation (for example: *I have* → *I've*)

◆ to show possession (*Danny told a joke* → *Danny's joke*).

Activity

Read the speech below. The words in blue should be turned into their abbreviated form. Write the abbreviations down.

I can not believe it. I really did not think I had a chance of winning. It is the greatest moment of my life. Of course you do not win an award like this on your own. There are so many others I would like to give my thanks to. First, huge hugs and kisses to my director. Steven is a remarkable man, he is just so dedicated. Then there is my stylist Candelabra; she has got such awesome talent with a mascara brush. I would also like to praise Stella, who is the greatest designer ever, and Lucille, who had a real job organising my hectic life for me. Last, of course, I would like to thank Mum and Dad; they are simply the best. And of course there is you, my adoring fans. You are the greatest. I love you all!

Peer-evaluation

Imagine that you have won an award. You might want to choose from one below or make up your own:

- Student of the year
- Sports personality of the year
- National spelling champion.

Write a speech giving thanks to those who have helped you. DO NOT include any abbreviations, just like the activity above.

When you have finished, swap your speech with a partner and abbreviate as many words as you can.

Apostrophes of possession

An apostrophe of possession shows that something belongs to, or is somehow linked with, something else.

- If the 'owning' noun is **singular**, add an apostrophe and 's': **'s**

Armando owns a Ferrari	→	Armando's Ferrari
There is an entrance to the stadium	→	the stadium's entrance
The comedian tells a joke	→	the comedian's joke

- If the 'owning' noun is **plural** (more than one), just add an apostrophe to the 's': **s'**

The nurses have a union	→	the nurses' union
The teachers have an office	→	the teachers' office

- **Irregular plurals** require an apostrophe and an 's' (like a singular noun) when they are the 'owner': **'s**

The children have a nursery	→	the children's nursery
The women have a toilet	→	the women's toilet

Activity 1

Look at the two boxes below. The first box contains 'owners', the second box contains things that are 'owned'. Pair the items from each box. Then write a sentence about the pairing. For example:

'owner' = car   'owned' = tyre. The **car's tyre** had a puncture.

Owners
car   teapot   victim   footballers
decorator   old lady   students
politician   warriors   rap star

Owned
party   battle-cry   paint   tyre
handbag   CD   spout   opinion
injury   luxury homes

HANDY HINTS

You must use an apostrophe to show possession, even when what is owned does not appear in the sentence, for example:

I'm going to Paul's after school.

The apostrophe is still needed because **Paul's** stands for **Paul's house**. Many shop names should have apostrophes but they often miss them out. **Debenhams** should really be spelled **Debenham's** as it stands for **Debenham's store**. What others can you spot like this?

Activity 2

The titles on these films have apostrophes missing. Write out the titles correctly.

Dads Army

National Lampoons Animal House

One Flew Over The Cuckoos Nest

WILLIAM SHAKESPEARES ROMEO AND JULIET

Monty Pythons Life Of Brian

Oceans Eleven

THE FLINTSTONES CHRISTMAS PARTY

Breakfast At Tiffanys

Peter Kays Phoenix Nights

Waynes World

The Simpsons Halloween Episodes

My Best Friends Wedding

Harry Potter And The Philosophers Stone

Billy Connollys World Tour Of Australia

A Bugs Life

Charlottes Web

A History Of The Champions League

Pirates Of The Caribbean: Dead Mans Chest

Dr. Seuss How The Grinch Stole Christmas

HANDY HINTS

Proper nouns that end in **s** can either end with an apostrophe and an **s** or just an apostrophe, for example:

Britney Spears's new CD   or   Britney Spears' new CD

Tom Hanks's latest film   or   Tom Hanks' latest film

Activity 3

Look at the photographs below. They contain real examples of apostrophe misuse. Write down the correct version of each sign.

a — Access restricted Saturday's only 7.30 am - 5.30 pm

b — ACCESS TO CHURCH STREET NCP CAR PARK LOCAL BUSINESS'S RESIDENTS

c — Dessert's ... ITALIAN PROFITTEROL cream & t... TIRAMI...

d — THERE ARE NO STRANGERS HERE, JUST FRIEND'S THAT HAVEN'T MET YET !!!

e — Family's dining are welcome until 6pm Thank you

f — Part Time Chef's / Cook's Required Must Have A Good Understanding Of English Please Apply Within

Activity 4

Read the following facts. Some of the apostrophes are in correct places, others are not. Write out every fact properly.

1 Elephant's are the only mammal that cant jump.

2 Like fingerprints, everyones tongue print's are different.

3 A hedgehogs heart sometimes beat's 300 times a minute.

4 Camels have three eyelids to protect them from sand storms.

5 Cow's milk cause's more allergies' than any other food.

6 Ostriches' eyes' are bigger than their brains'.

7 Banana's arent really fruits, they're berries.

8 Mens nose's and ears never stop growing.

9 Dont burp or sneeze in Churches' in Nebraska, USA: its against the law!

10 Theres a Stockholm restaurant that only sell's garlic products. It's even got garlic cheesecake!

Hyphens

RULES

- Hyphens are used to join two or more words to make a new word, for example:

  fun-loving person
  blue-eyed boy

- Hyphens can make a big difference to the meaning of a sentence as in:

  No smoking restrictions (smoking IS allowed)
  No-smoking restrictions (smoking IS NOT allowed)

HANDY HINTS

Hyphens are used to join words that are broken between the end of one line of writing and the start of the next. Do not confuse this way of saving space on a page with the creation of new words and meanings.

Activity

Explain the different meanings created by the hyphens below. To show you understand the difference, write an example that uses each one.

1 resign   and re-sign

2 man eating tiger   and man-eating tiger

3 reserve   and re-serve

4 recover   and re-cover

5 used car salesman   and used-car salesman

6 50 year-old puppies   and 50-year-old puppies

How many words?

Be careful not to join two separate words together and write them as one word. Do not write two separate words when only one is needed.

Activity

Work with a partner to decide which of the following sentences is correct.

1 There's a lot of noise.   or There's alot of noise.

2 I had already finished.   or I had all ready finished.

3 My room is upstairs.   or My room is up stairs.

4 Move a bit to the left.   or Move abit to the left.

5 I'm going aswell.   or I'm going as well.

6 She's infront of me.   or She's in front of me.

7 Noone will talk to me.   or No one will talk to me.

8 It's underneath the rug.   or It's under neath the rug.

Spelling and punctuation: self-test

Complete the tests below. When you have finished, your teacher will have the answers to check against.

Self-test 1 : Capital letters

Write out the following sentences putting in the missing capital letters.

1 if i put a coin in a glass of pepsi on tuesday, will it be shiny by wednesday?
2 did you know there is a city called smackover in arkansas, usa?
3 in the united states and france, one out of every three families has a pet dog.
4 the wheelbarrow, kites and fireworks were invented by the chinese.
5 the 71 million packets of biscuits sold every year by united biscuits, owner of mcvitie's, creates 125 tons of crumbs.
6 all the smarties eaten in a year would stretch around the Earth's equator nearly three times.
7 When he was the american president, george w bush once said, "most imports are from outside of the country."
8 a channel 4 poll voted *the simpsons* as the greatest cartoon of all time.
9 in 1884 dr hervey d thatcher invented the milk bottle. in 1971 prime minister margaret thatcher earned the nickname of milk-snatcher.
10 the name of wendy was invented for the book *peter pan*, by jm barrie.

Self-test 2 : Capital letters

Write out the following sentences putting in the missing capital letters.

1 after being given detention on monday, sandeep snarled, "i hate mr godkin. he's evil."
2 the nhs is always very busy during the period around bonfire night.
3 computer games have come a long way since space invaders and pac-man.
4 george asked, "can we go to kfc now that i've finished my homework?"
5 "because he has antlers at christmas, rudolph must be a girl!" laughed ali.
6 "you should see these old pictures of my dad. look at his hair," sniggered sam.
7 over a million people have attended garden parties at buckingham palace during the reign of queen elizabeth II.
8 "come on, i'm starving. is that tesco near you open 24 hours a day?' asked reese.
9 "the camp site we stayed on had lots of french and dutch tourists staying there," said aaron.
10 the teacher, mrs nadal, explained that the spanish trip was only for sixth form students.

Self-test 3 : Apostrophes

Make sense of these sentences by putting in the correct apostrophes.

1 Gemmas patience was running out with Lukes immature behaviour.
2 "My phones been nicked, Im gutted," sighed Alex.
3 I cant understand why those companies logos are identical.
4 Youll never get a decent grade when youre behaving like a real loser.
5 It was the boys fault the windows were smashed.

Self-test **3** : Apostrophes (continued)

6 "Shes going to be there later. Ill see you at Lees," said Oli.

7 Mr Morris lessons are painfully boring. Hes an awful teacher.

8 Many visitors turned up and the demonstrations were a great success.

9 "Your cars a piece of junk," laughed Charlie. "Itll never pass its MOT."

10 If youre travelling by plane, dont leave your luggage unattended.

Self-test **4** : Apostrophes

Make sense of these sentences by putting in the correct apostrophes.

1 "Thats Kims phone. Shes been looking everywhere for it," said Jay.

2 "Im afraid the hard-drives had it," said the technician.

3 Hows your spelling coming on? With this books help you ought to improve.

4 The teams attitude was appalling. Theyd given up after the refs poor decision.

5 Theyre not coming with us. Theyll cause trouble and guess wholl get blamed as well?

6 "Its the peoples choice who they elect," declared the Prime Minister.

7 'Chris, lets get a MacDonalds and go. Itll be a laugh if were early," said Ashley.

8 The cows tongues are covered in blisters. Do you think theyve got a disease?

9 I wont go, ive no reason to. Ill be embarrassed wont I?

10 The drive-throughs intercom was terrible. They couldnt hear your order.

Self-test **5** : General punctuation

This paragraph covers all the rules in Unit 7. Write it out correctly.

"youve got to be kidding, its the most boring game in the world," sighed ed.

"well that's what were doing for Lewis birthday bash. he wants to spend the day at a cricket match." the unfortunate ed did'nt know whether to laugh or cry.

"this has got to be your mates doing hasn't it? Youll have put them up to this, i reckon," he said, accusingly. ian looked a little guilty as he replied.

"well…i may have had a bit to do with it. i suppose i just might have mentioned that i can get free ticket's, and it is an england versus australia game. Theyre great to watch."

ed was becoming angry. "For you perhaps, but itll be a nightmare for everyone else. and its on a Saturday. well be bored to death. So how many peoples fun have you ruined with this idea?" ian decided to take a different approach.

"Therell be about twenty-odd mates going and ive got it all sorted. Weve got the best seat's; the views brilliant. All the foods free, because marks uncle works for sky tv and he can get us into the hospitality suite." eds face brightened at the mention of free food. "ive even got us a lift to and from the ground from Mick in his parents car."

Well done for the answers you got right! If you got any wrong, go back to the part of the unit that will help you and work through the activities again. Your teacher also has additional activities to help you.

OBJECTIVES

This unit will help you to understand some of the more unusual features of spelling. By the end of this unit you will be able to:

- choose correctly between **homophones**
- understand how **silent letters** work
- recognise when words are misspelled on purpose.

Homophones

Homophones are words that sound the same but have different spellings and meanings, for example:

brake (*slow down*)	→	break (*damage*)
grown (*got bigger*)	→	groan (*complain*)
sale (*things to buy*)	→	sail (*on a boat*)
leak (*not water-tight*)	→	leek (*vegetable*)

Activity 1

Read the sentences below. Choose the correct word from the box so that the sentence makes sense.

1 There's a hole in the _____ where a cold _____ is blowing in.

2 Don't _____ from shops; you'll get _____ by store detectives.

3 The price of that tomato _____ is very _____ .

4 After that long walk my _____ are extremely _____ .

5 I don't really like black _____ , only _____ ones.

cheap / cheep	draught / draft	steel / steal
jeans / genes	blue / blew	caught / court
saw / sore	sauce / source	
flaw / floor	feat / feet	

Activity 2

In the box above there are ten words you did not use in Activity 1. Write a sentence for each of them to show you understand its meaning. Use a dictionary to find the meaning of any words you do not understand.

HANDY HINT

Homophones cause problems with computer spellchecks. A computer spellcheck will only tell you if a word is spelled incorrectly. It will not correct the mistake if you have chosen the wrong word. A computer spellcheck would not find any mistakes in the following passage.

Ewe kneed two bee very care full with spell cheques. Eye am a frayed they own lee sea reel spelling miss steaks; they do knot no if ewe have putt the wrong word. They are sup posed two save thyme but if ewe do knot luck close lea ewe cud miss sum errors like these. It is all ways better two ewes yaw own brain.

Activity 3

Explain the difference between the following words. Write a sentence for each word to show you understand its meaning.

father / farther	stalk / stork
dew / due	swat / swot
pause / paws / pores / pours	mare / mayor
hall / haul	medal / meddle
bite / byte	

Activity 4

Read the following letter. It contains many examples of the wrong homophone being used. Write out the article correctly.

Dear Sir,

Eye have the knead to right too you following a pane full experience I suffered in yaw restaurant last weak.

I new things whirr going to be pore write from the start as the table was extremely dirty. The bread on the table did not luck fresh. Inn fact I broke a tooth when I tried to byte it. The mane coarse was knot cooked properly because the stake was roar. It also tuck an our too arrive. The pairs in the suite were still frozen. The whine tasted like vinegar and the staff ignored my complaints.

I have bean to many restaurants awl over the whirled, butt I have never scene such dreadful food. Do you think a guessed should be treated like this? Wood you putt up with such awful service? Everything I eight maid me want to bee sick.

I wood be grate full four a full explanation as soon as possible.

Yours faithfully,

'there', 'their' and 'they're'

- **'there'** has two uses.
  1 It shows a place, for example: *My friend is over* **there**.
  2 It is also used with *verbs*, for example: **There** *is my friend*.
- **'their'** means 'belonging to them', for example: *That is* **their** *car*.
- **'they're'** is an **abbreviation** for 'they are', for example:
  They're *talking to my friend*.

Activity

Write out these sentences again, correctly using **there**, **they're** or **their**.

1 If that's _____ idea of a good time, _____ crazy?

2 If _____ was a different route, _____ information was incorrect.

3 _____ looking in the wrong place, it's over _____ .

4 If _____ well-behaved, I'll increase _____ pocket money soon.

5 I'll take _____ photographs when _____ looking this way.

'its' and 'it's'

Activity

Write out these sentences again, correctly using **its** or **it's**.

1 Because the house is damp, ____ going to lose some of ____ value.

2 ____ a simple game but only when you know ____ rules.

3 My laptop lost ____ Internet connection so ____ been difficult to work.

4 ____ going to take a while but I'll let you know when ____ finished.

5 ____ poor service meant the hotel couldn't improve ____ reputation.

If you have problems using **there**, **they're** and **their**, ask yourself these questions before you choose which one to write.

- Would 'they are' make sense in your writing? If so, choose **they're**.
- Is something owned by 'them'? If so, choose **their**.
- If neither of the above seems right, choose **there**.

- **its** means 'belonging to it', for example: *The engine lost* **its** *power*.
- **it's** is an abbreviation for 'it is' or 'it has', for example: **It's** *time to go*.

'to', 'too' and 'two'; 'your' and 'you're' *IWB*

- **to** has two meanings.
  1 It shows the direction 'towards', for example: *I'm going **to** school.*
  2 It can also be used with a verb to make the infinitive, for example: *I need **to** have something to eat.*

- **too** has two meanings.
  1 It means 'also' or 'as well', for example: *I'd like some crisps **too**.*
  2 It also means an excess or a surplus (too much), for example: *It was **too** easy.*

- **two** always means the number 2, for example: *There are **two** lessons to go.*

- **your** means 'belonging to you', for example: *Is that **your** bag?*

- **you're** is an abbreviation for 'you are', for example: *I think **you're** right.*

Activity 1

Write out these sentences. Fill in the gaps with **to**, **too** or **two**.

1 If you want ____ feel ill, drink ____ many milkshakes.

2 She needed ____ attempts ____ get the right answer.

3 Whenever I go ____ see friends, my sister has ____ come ____ .

4 It's far ____ early for me ____ do anything energetic.

5 She needs ____ understand that it's happened ____ often.

6 We need ____ get there by ____ o'clock.

7 Those directions ____ the park aren't ____ clear.

8 I'm going ____ the doctor as I can't get ____ sleep at night.

9 If you want ____ be successful, learn ____ organise yourself.

10 The library was ____ quiet for Sarah; she wanted ____ giggle!

Activity 2

Write out these sentences. Fill in the gaps with **your** or **you're**.

1 To improve _____ image, _____ going to have to work very hard.

2 _____ best friend is one _____ sure you can trust.

3 You'll find _____ bag underneath _____ bed.

4 I hope _____ certain that it wasn't _____ fault.

5 I think _____ wrong. _____ English teacher is much better than mine.

6 When _____ in a better mood you can have _____ pocket money.

7 If _____ listening carefully _____ going to understand more.

8 _____ biggest fault is _____ always late.

9 _____ being very generous but the credit is all _____s.

10 I would like _____ opinion if _____ sure you have the time.

'past' and 'passed'

- **passed** has different meanings.
  1. It can mean 'went by', for example: She **passed** the shop without going in.
  2. It can mean 'transferred', 'exchanged', 'gave', for example: He **passed** the baton to the next runner.
  3. It can mean 'agreed to', for example: The new law was **passed** after a vote.
  4. It can mean 'got through', for example: They all **passed** the exam with distinction.
- **past** also has different uses.
  1. It can mean 'beyond', for example: He swam **past** the dangerous reef.
  2. It can mean a time, for example: It's half-**past** three.
  3. It can mean 'in times gone by', for example: They believed in witches in the **past**.

Activity 1

Write a sentence for every different meaning of **passed** and **past** from the rule box above. You should write seven sentences. With a partner, check you have both used the words correctly.

Activity 2

Write out the sentences below, filling in the gaps correctly with **past** or **passed**. When you have finished, check your answers with a partner.

1. A worried look _____ between them as they walked _____ the hospital.
2. It's nearly a quarter _____four. If he'd _____ he'd have rung by now.
3. He strolled _____ his old home without sorrow. The heartache was firmly in the _____ now.
4. He _____ ten GCSEs, all with top grades.
5. I _____ the shop without realising it.

'off' and 'of'

- **off** means the opposite of 'on', for example: Turn the radio **off**. It can also mean 'away' or 'in motion', for example: They ran **off**.
- **of** has many meanings. If you don't mean 'away', 'in motion' or the opposite of 'on', use **of**!

Activity 1

Write out the sentences below, filling in the gaps correctly with **off** or **of**. When you have finished, check your answers with a partner.

1. He got ____ the bus and grabbed a cup ____ coffee.
2. One ____ the best ways ____ getting slim is to work ____ the calories with exercise.
3. Turning things ____ at the mains will save lots ____ money.
4. On the fifth ____ November you'll hear many fireworks going ____ .
5. You're out ____ luck: the milk has gone ____ .

Activity 2

Write around 100 words about your school. Include as many **deliberate** mistakes with homophones as you can. Then swap your work with a partner. How many 'mistakes' did they make?

Silent letters

Silent letters appear in the spelling of words, but are not heard when the words are spoken aloud.

> wi**t**ch   **k**nitting   yol**k**
> cush**i**on   com**b**   **p**sycho

Activity 1

Read the letter of complaint opposite. All the silent letters have been missed out of the words in red. Write the words out correctly.

Activity 2

Read the sentences below. All the silent letters have been missed out of the words in red. Write out the words correctly.

1 The church organist was playing a **solem hym**.

2 I'm not so **hansome** now I've got so many **rinkles**.

3 I often go **climing** at the weekend.

4 The **cuboard** was full of **biscit crums**.

5 **nock** three times and the **casle gard** will let you pass.

Dear Madam,

Last **Wenesday** I spoke to one of your staff concerning **wen** my **morgage** would be confirmed. I spent an **our** being reassured that as soon as I **sined** the papers everything would be completed by the start of **Febuary**. The letter I **receved** today now says that early **autum** is the best I can expect. Do you **now wy** this is? The owners of the **bilding** I want to buy are becoming impatient and I feel **gilty** about messing them about.

Please **rite** immediately as I'm having **douts** about the **hole** thing.

Yours faithfully,

Misc-spell-aneous! Self-tests

Complete the tests below. When you have finished, your teacher will have the answers to check against.

Self-test : Homophones

Choose the correct word in blue for the sentence to make sense. Write down the complete sentence.

1 You're not **aloud/allowed** in there.
2 The window **pane/pain** was cracked.
3 I **heard/herd** a strange noise.
4 I think I've got **flu/flew**.
5 I **made/maid** a real fuss.
6 The chocolate **moose/mousse** is great.
7 He **nose/knows** what you mean.
8 A loaf of **bred/bread**.
9 I need to **flea/flee** the country.
10 The postman brings the **mail/male**.

Self-test 2 : Homophones

Choose the correct word in red for the sentence to make sense. Write down the complete sentence.

1 It was a **miner/minor** accident.
2 They had a glass of **wine/whine**.
3 My **hair/hare** is a mess.
4 **Which/Witch** lesson is next?
5 A queen sits on a **throne/thrown**.
6 That was a **week/weak** effort.
7 Karate is a **martial/marshal** art.
8 Send up a distress **flair/flare**.
9 I play **bass/base** guitar.
10 I'm going to **die/dye** my hair.

Self-test 3 : Homophones

Choose the correct word in green for the sentence to make sense. Write down the complete sentence.

1 A **hare/hair** looks similar to a rabbit.
2 The stuntman **sighed/side** with relief.
3 The soldiers went back to their **base/bass**.
4 The prison **cell/sell** didn't look cosy.
5 She **rode/road** a white stallion.
6 I have changed my **mined/mind**.
7 How much **profit/prophet** did you make?
8 I need to **hire/higher** a car.
9 There's a crack in the **sealing/ceiling**.
10 Make sure you've **packed/pact** your case.

Self-test 4 : Homophones

Choose the correct word in purple for the sentence to make sense.
Write down the complete sentence.

1 You look **warn/worn** out.

2 I **billed/build** houses for a living.

3 The bells were **rung/wrung** loudly.

4 I paid him a **compliment/complement**.

5 The **creek/creak** came from the old door.

6 The **bald/bawled** man wore a wig.

7 The colours were bright and **bold/bowled**.

8 Only three **laps/lapse** to go.

9 I **guessed/guest** the answer.

10 The red **rows/rose** smelled delightful.

Self-test 5 : Silent letters

Write out the words in red with their missing silent letter.

1 You got that **anser** correct.

2 You need a **plumer** to fix that leak.

3 That's a very sharp **nife**.

4 **Fasen** all your shirt buttons.

5 After summer comes **autum**.

6 That **hege** needs trimming.

7 My feet are **num** with cold.

8 Fresh **samon** tastes better than tinned.

9 Those jeans are so out of **fashon**.

10 I **rote** you a letter.

Self-test 6 : Silent letters

Write out the words in blue with their missing silent letter.

1 I **new** I was right.

2 I have paid off my **dets**.

3 I could **desin** a better car than that.

4 I need to **rap** that present.

5 I could have **neumonia**.

6 I must **lisen** more carefully.

7 I can play **gitar**.

8 I have hurt my **rist**.

9 I'm as white as a **gost**.

10 I have a blister on my **tonge**.

Well done for the answers you got right! If you got any wrong, go back to the part of the unit that will help you and work through the activities again. Your teacher also has additional activities to help you.

THE SPELLING CHALLENGE

OBJECTIVES

This unit will help you to spell correctly words that are commonly used.
If you are unsure what a word means, look it up in a dictionary or check with your teacher.

The first FIVE sections are words connected with these school subjects: English, Mathematics, Technology, Science and Humanities. There are three levels of difficulty: bronze, silver and gold.

1 Get a friend to test your spelling of each word.

2 For each word that you have spelled correctly: WELL DONE! Note down the numbers of the words you have spelled incorrectly.

3 Use the strategies in Unit 1 to learn the spellings you got wrong.

4 Get a friend to test you again. If you have spelled enough words correctly, move on to the next level.

Go for GOLD in each subject!

English

BRONZE AWARD (you must get at least 27 out of 30 to get the award)

1	verb	7	theme	13	scene	19	noun	25	speech
2	adverb	8	image	14	slang	20	drama	26	fact
3	sonnet	9	write	15	colon	21	discuss	27	contrast
4	ballad	10	ode	16	vowel	22	pun	28	draft
5	comma	11	quote	17	capital	23	poem	29	inform
6	comment	12	argue	18	blurb	24	prose	30	media

SILVER AWARD (you must get at least 45 out of 50 to get the award)

1	fiction	11	irony	21	rhyme	31	hyphen	41	analogy
2	emotion	12	summary	22	genre	32	narrative	42	accent
3	preposition	13	empathy	23	anecdote	33	antonym	43	stanza
4	opinion	14	imply	24	feature	34	article	44	extract
5	critical	15	clause	25	character	35	grammar	45	tabloid
6	literal	16	farce	26	phrase	36	singular	46	proverb
7	acrostic	17	simile	27	narrator	37	suffix	47	legend
8	symbolic	18	plural	28	audience	38	prefix	48	couplet
9	dialect	19	adjective	29	paragraph	39	insight	49	tragedy
10	parody	20	myth	30	persuade	40	pronoun	50	Shakespeare

GOLD AWARD (you must get at least 25 out of 30 to get the award)

1	abbreviation	7	characteristic	13	dialogue	19	euphemism	25	personification
2	alliteration	8	monologue	14	onomatopoeia	20	persuasive	26	rhetorical
3	conjunction	9	caricature	15	quotation	21	enjambment	27	dialogue
4	exclamation	10	rhythmical	16	literature	22	soliloquy	28	consonant
5	interjection	11	syllable	17	literacy	23	ambiguous	29	autobiography
6	punctuation	12	haiku	18	homophone	24	synonym	30	metaphor

Mathematics

BRONZE AWARD (you must get at least 27 out of 30 to get the award)

1	acute	7	area	13	degree	19	regular	25	equal
2	cosine	8	depth	14	factor	20	helix	26	axis
3	convex	9	compass	15	length	21	cubic	27	metre
4	litre	10	angle	16	pentagon	22	polygon	28	similar
5	square	11	chance	17	wrong	23	sine	29	volume
6	minus	12	width	18	vector	24	vertex	30	scale

SILVER AWARD (you must get at least 55 out of 60 to get the award)

1	calculate	13	centimetre	25	diagonal	37	dimension	49	height
2	horizontal	14	inverse	26	kilometre	38	adjacent	50	average
3	value	15	cylinder	27	distribution	39	ratio	51	isometric
4	latitude	16	longitude	28	measure	40	algebra	52	diameter
5	divide	17	elevation	29	gradient	41	heptagon	53	sphere
6	median	18	weight	30	capacity	42	octagon	54	converge
7	decagon	19	significant	31	ellipse	43	estimate	55	pyramid
8	fraction	20	graph	32	hexagon	44	inclination	56	linear
9	matrix	21	bearing	33	Celsius	45	circle	57	collate
10	validity	22	coordinate	34	decimal	46	deviation	58	digit
11	maximum	23	millimetre	35	minimum	47	negative	59	frequency
12	relative	24	scalene	36	tangent	48	vertices	60	prism

GOLD AWARD (you must get at least 21 out of 25 to get the award)

1	concentric	6	correlation	11	questionnaire	16	dodecagon	21	quadrilateral
2	percentage	7	symmetrical	12	trapezium	17	circumference	22	Pythagoras
3	statistical	8	tessellation	13	denominator	18	multiplication	23	simultaneous
4	equilateral	9	Fahrenheit	14	hypotenuse	19	isosceles	24	geometrical
5	parallelogram	10	subtraction	15	coefficient	20	trigonometry	25	perpendicular

Technology

BRONZE AWARD (you must get at least 19 out of 20 to get the award)

1	computer	5	display	9	mouse	13	mobile	17	format
2	printer	6	safety	10	surface	14	grain	18	diet
3	scanner	7	pixel	11	force	15	icon	19	brief
4	colour	8	mineral	12	menu	16	fashion	20	vitamin

SILVER AWARD (you must get at least 18 out of 20 to get the award)

1	investigation	5	fibre	9	assemble	13	outcome	17	graphics
2	presentation	6	industrial	10	lathe	14	indicate	18	gluten
3	function	7	design	11	vegetable	15	criteria	19	protein
4	suitability	8	research	12	packaging	16	dyeing	20	preview

GOLD AWARD (you must get at least 17 out of 20 to get the award)

1	specification	5	efficiency	9	appearance	13	embroidery	17	elasticity
2	acceleration	6	implement	10	adjustable	14	laminate	18	diagram
3	evaluation	7	component	11	analyse	15	approximately	19	quantify
4	limitations	8	nutrients	12	aerodynamic	16	temperature	20	carbohydrate

Science

BRONZE AWARD (you must get at least 23 out of 25 to get the award)

1 acid	6 funnel	11 beaker	16 spore	21 artery
2 plasma	7 tripod	12 digest	17 force	22 density
3 sensor	8 joule	13 watt	18 dilute	23 proton
4 element	9 electron	14 alcohol	19 solvent	24 voltage
5 fungus	10 alloy	15 extinct	20 vein	25 energy

SILVER AWARD (you must get at least 40 out of 45 to get the award)

1 alkaline	10 bacteria	19 oxygen	28 nuclear	37 physics
2 medicine	11 molecule	20 nucleus	29 experiment	38 gravity
3 humidity	12 particle	21 electricity	30 liquid	39 muscle
4 observation	13 structure	22 genetic	31 resistor	40 apparatus
5 chemistry	14 catalyst	23 pipette	32 emulsion	41 friction
6 microscope	15 insulator	24 hydrogen	33 crystal	42 neutron
7 periodic	16 biology	25 combustion	34 corrosive	43 dissolve
8 soluble	17 kinetic	26 disease	35 skeleton	44 organism
9 suspension	18 hygiene	27 evaporation	36 formula	45 stomach

GOLD AWARD (you must get at least 16 out of 20 to get the award)

1 thermometer	5 vaccine	9 diaphragm	13 germination	17 chromatography
2 centrifuge	6 fertilisation	10 electromagnet	14 biodegradable	18 igneous
3 environment	7 electrolysis	11 photosynthesis	15 concentration	19 impermeable
4 metabolism	8 condensation	12 chromosome	16 chlorophyll	20 laboratory

Humanities

BRONZE AWARD (you must get at least 19 out of 20 to get the award)

1 bible	5 Hindu	9 faith	13 rite	17 saint
2 cause	6 atlas	10 desert	14 flood	18 iceberg
3 plain	7 pulpit	11 scale	15 gospel	19 moral
4 village	8 vicar	12 church	16 fault	20 valley

SILVER AWARD (you must get at least 31 out of 35 to get the award)

1 climate	8 condensation	15 erosion	22 continent	29 cyclone
2 spirit	9 racial	16 industry	23 depression	30 contour
3 population	10 primary	17 abortion	24 refuge	31 sediment
4 settlement	11 typhoon	18 communist	25 civilisation	32 secondary
5 miracle	12 regional	19 parable	26 missionary	33 century
6 hurricane	13 monarch	20 prayer	27 prophet	34 decade
7 conurbation	14 irrigation	21 tourism	28 suburb	35 generation

GOLD AWARD (you must get at least 22 out of 25 to get the award)

1 reference	6 manufacturing	11 precipitation	16 agricultural	21 Buddhist
2 Sikh	7 commandment	12 crucify	17 martyr	22 archaeology
3 carboniferous	8 prejudice	13 propaganda	18 reformation	23 conscience
4 millennium	9 conclusion	14 pacifism	19 parliament	24 government
5 atheism	10 euthanasia	15 secularisation	20 synagogue	25 contraception

Common mistakes

The following pages contain the words that are most commonly spelled incorrectly. Some words are followed by a word in brackets to avoid confusing the word with another sounding the same. The tests increase in difficulty.

Test 1

This test comes from the **most commonly used** words in the English language. You should make sure you can spell ALL of these words.

1	blue	11	write (pen)	21	always	31	read (book)	41	why
2	could	12	once	22	when	32	found	42	about
3	what	13	before	23	again	33	because	43	were
4	does	14	said	24	only	34	clean	44	goes
5	right (not left)	15	three	25	better	35	upon	45	these
6	where (question)	16	would	26	every	36	eight (number)	46	pretty
7	funny	17	together	27	today	37	please	47	fly
8	thank	18	four (number)	28	myself	38	round	48	those
9	laugh	19	work	29	going	39	black	49	start
10	light	20	hurt	30	both	40	white	50	which (question)

Test 2

1	people	5	teacher	9	please	13	purple	17	train
2	brother	6	children	10	nail	14	watch	18	wheel
3	night	7	story	11	helpful	15	giving	19	catch
4	chair	8	year	12	great	16	iron	20	about

Test 3

1	stopped	5	across	9	rabbit	13	straight	17	afraid
2	racing	6	afternoon	10	afraid	14	doctor	18	doesn't
3	really	7	almost	11	knife	15	another	19	laugh
4	everyone	8	balloon	12	because	16	scratch	20	scream

Test 4

1	behind	5	lose	9	second	13	touch	17	birthday
2	flies	6	match	10	trouble	14	friend	18	should
3	build	7	mouth	11	voice	15	guess	19	carries
4	whole	8	cloud	12	piece	16	stairs	20	quickly

Test 5

1	caught	5	damage	9	address	13	interested	17	although
2	answer	6	disappear	10	quite	14	quiet	18	believe
3	knocked	7	remember	11	engine	15	enough	19	exciting
4	let's	8	library	12	breath	16	listen	20	sauce

Test 6

1 centre	5 catch	9 whistle	13 changing	17 choice
2 clothing	6 ocean	10 written	14 squeeze	18 cousin
3 awful	7 helpful	11 until	15 happened	19 guard
4 highest	8 guest	12 action	16 decided	20 pleasant

Test 7

1 stomach	5 delicious	9 suggest	13 powerful	17 prejudiced
2 surprise	6 attach	10 imagine	14 attention	18 disappoint
3 question	7 beginning	11 represent	15 manufacture	19 treatment
4 memories	8 celebration	12 chocolate	16 favourite	20 fuel

Test 8

1 science	5 schedule	9 sincerely	13 country	17 government
2 wonderful	6 environment	10 graphic	14 uncovered	18 worried
3 absence	7 misunderstand	11 accidentally	15 resource	19 ability
4 contribute	8 achievement	12 adventure	16 neighbour	20 dangerous

Test 9

1 addresses	5 muscle	9 scissors	13 ambulance	17 definite
2 shoulder	6 coupon	10 separately	14 governor	18 decoration
3 gracious	7 decisive	11 handsome	15 appreciate	19 happiness
4 headache	8 passenger	12 assignment	16 determine	20 description

Test 10

1 heroes	5 disastrous	9 discriminate	13 beautifully	17 distributed
2 improvement	6 independent	10 maintenance	14 emptiness	18 knowledge
3 enormously	7 vacuum	11 excitement	15 experience	19 probably
4 accomplishment	8 exceptional	12 existence	16 acquire	20 fluid

Test 11

1 unnecessary	5 embarrassment	9 harassment	13 mysterious	17 significance
2 fascinating	6 committee	10 nervously	14 frequently	18 occupation
3 civilisation	7 comprehension	11 courageous	15 considerable	19 succeeded
4 successfully	8 poisonous	12 criminal	16 inaccurate	20 symphony

Test 12

1 permanent	5 anniversary	9 judgement	13 transferred	17 preferred
2 questionnaire	6 reasonable	10 involvement	14 encouragement	18 attitude
3 authorisation	7 merchandise	11 recommendation	15 receipt	19 vegetable
4 vaccinate	8 league	12 association	16 assistance	20 pronunciation

Test 13

1 desiccate	5 ecstasy	9 millennium	13 accommodate	17 irresistible
2 liaison	6 definitely	10 occurrence	14 cemetery	18 inoculate
3 sacrilegious	7 weird	11 applicable	15 acknowledgement	19 conscientiously
4 predominantly	8 foreigner	12 miscellaneous	16 hypothesis	20 pneumonia

Diagnostic tests– Answers

Diagnostic test 1: Plurals

Check your answers against the correct options.

1 frames	**14** journeys	**27** cables	**40** ceremonies
2 wolves	**15** qualities	**28** people	**41** criteria
3 hairbrushes	**16** bluffs	**29** pianos	**42** infernos
4 bailiffs	**17** fungi	**30** crises	**43** shelves
5 banjos	**18** taxes	**31** novelties	**44** witnesses
6 firemen	**19** feet	**32** policies	**45** bakeries
7 bellies	**20** straps	**33** scruffs	**46** scratches
8 curtains	**21** cliffs	**34** bleaches	**47** indexes
9 apples	**22** hamsters	**35** stresses	**48** designs
10 pictures	**23** counties	**36** elbows	**49** casualties
11 reefs	**24** thieves	**37** mottos or mottoes	**50** species
12 bricks	**25** rodeos	**38** leaves	
13 mice	**26** batteries	**39** trout	

Now use this table to show which part of Unit 3: Plurals can help you.

Mistakes on numbers	Unit 3: Plurals	Activities
1, 3, 8, 9, 10, 12, 18, 20, 22, 27, 34, 35, 36, 44, 46, 47, 48	When to add 's' or 'es' pages 30–31	1, 2
2, 4, 11, 16, 21, 24, 33, 38, 43	Words ending in 'f', 'ff' or 'fe' page 32	Activity (no number)
7, 14, 15, 23, 26, 31, 32, 40, 45, 49	Words ending in 'y' pages 33–34	1, 2, 3
5, 25, 29, 37, 42	Words ending in 'o' page 35	Activity (no number)
6, 13, 17, 19, 28, 30, 39, 41, 50	Irregular plurals page 35	1, 2

Diagnostic test 2: Spelling and punctuation

Check your answers carefully against the sentences below.

1 He heard his friend call, "See you in September, Tom."
2 She wears out-of-date clothes but is a fun-loving person.
3 I'm not sure if it's right. It doesn't look as if I've done it properly.
4 All of the supporters' shouting and cheering was extremely loud.
5 There was a programme about the RAF on TV last night.
6 Peter and Sanjit went to a Bonfire Night display in York.
7 If I know Marcia, I bet she knows the title of the new Madonna CD.
8 There are a lot of people who injure themselves running.
9 If Kelly's there it'll mean trouble. She doesn't get on well with Ellen's friends.
10 They turned as he asked, "Fancy coming to KFC? My treat? I'm feeling generous."
11 That doesn't belong to you. I'm sure it's David's.
12 Only when he arrived in school did he remember about the French test.
13 When we're there we'll make sure everything's OK.
14 If you're unsure about it, you'd better check with Emily's dad.
15 "When the English play Australia, they always get thrashed," laughed Shane.

Now use this table to show which part of Unit 7: Spelling and Punctuation can help you.

Mistakes on numbers	Unit 7: Spelling and punctuation	Activities
1, 5, 6, 7, 10, 11, 12, 14, 15	Capital letters pages 81–82	1, 2, 3
3, 9, 10, 11, 13, 14	Apostrophes of abbreviation page 83	Activity (no number)
4, 9, 11, 14	Apostrophes of possession page 84–86	1, 2, 3, 4
2	Hyphens page 87	Activity (no number)
8	How many words? page 87	Activity (no number)

Diagnostic test 3: Homophones and silent letters

Check your answers carefully against the correct spellings.

1 **Cheap** fireworks are dangerous and should **be banned**.
2 My **limbs** ache but I don't **know whether** it's serious.
3 I drove **past** the place where I **passed** my driving test.
4 I used some **subtle** hints to **soften** the news.
5 With a little more **insight** I wouldn't have needed a **loan**.
6 I'm sure **you're** right, so I'll take your advice.
7 We **need** to decide **where** to go next **time**.
8 If you have **too** much fatty food, you may have **to** cut it down.
9 You're **wrong**, so don't get your **knickers** in a twist!
10 **I saw you** walk **through** that puddle.
11 Take your coat **off**. It's the middle of summer.
12 I wish I'd **seen** that **new** film.

Now use this table to show which part of Unit 8: Misc-spell-aneous can help you.

Mistakes on numbers	Unit 8: Misc-spell-aneous!	Activities
1, 5, 7, 10, 12	Homophones pages 90–91	1, 2, 3, 4
8	'to', 'too' and 'two' page 93	1
6	'your' and 'you're' page 93	2
3	'past' and 'passed' page 94	1, 2
11	'off' and 'of' page 94	1
2, 4, 9	Silent letters page 95	1, 2

Diagnostic test 4: Soft letter sounds

Check your answers against the correct options.

1 cemetery	9 specimen	17 situation	25 cider
2 terrace	10 crevice	18 engine	26 infancy
3 generate	11 dunce	19 jealous	27 gesture
4 fanciful	12 fireplace	20 currency	28 crucify
5 dismiss	13 decimal	21 bandage	29 adhesive
6 segment	14 necklace	22 knowledge	30 gymnastics
7 sponge	15 cynical	23 cartridge	
8 delicacy	16 accomplice	24 apprentice	

Now use this table to show which part of Unit 5: Common letter patterns can help you.

Mistakes on numbers	Unit 5: Common letter patterns	Activities
2, 5, 6, 10, 14, 16, 17, 24, 29	Soft 'c' spellings page 51	1, 2, 3, 4
1, 4, 8, 9, 11, 12, 13, 15, 20, 25, 26, 28	Soft 'cy', 'ce' and 'ci' spellings page 52	1, 2
3, 18, 19, 27, 30	Soft 'g' spellings page 53	1, 2
7, 21, 22, 23	'ge' and 'dge' endings page 54	Activity (no number)

Diagnostic test 5: Common letter patterns

Check your answers against the correct letter patterns.

1 their	9 conceive	17 earphones	25 holograph
2 glacier	10 funnel	18 review	26 sleigh
3 achieve	11 relieved	19 shield	27 receivership
4 briefcase	12 oriental	20 fiend	28 briefing
5 emphasis	13 phase	21 physical	29 grievous
6 field	14 height	22 refund	30 viewer
7 trophy	15 conscience	23 wield	
8 sufficient	16 receive	24 perceive	

Now use this table to show which part of Unit 5: Common letter patterns can help you.

Mistakes on numbers	Unit 5: Common letter patterns	Activities
5, 7, 10, 13, 17, 21, 22, 25	'ph' words page 55	1, 2
1, 2, 3, 4, 6, 8, 9, 11, 12, 14, 15, 16, 18, 19, 20, 23, 24, 26, 27, 28, 29, 30	'ei' or 'ie' spellings? pages 56–57	1, 2, 3, 4

Diagnostic test 6: Common letter patterns

Check your answers against the correct letter patterns.

1 mechanic	13 squat	25 chassis	37 queer
2 branch	14 luxury	26 munch	38 inequality
3 wretch	15 liquid	27 bewitched	39 squeak
4 gorgeous	16 warmth	28 anxious	40 wardrobe
5 powder	17 devout	29 dubious	41 architect
6 chef	18 foundation	30 bound	42 search
7 wrench	19 cliché	31 clout	43 equator
8 approach	20 matches	32 worth	44 county
9 hound	21 couch	33 wonder	45 enquire
10 shepherd	22 chasm	34 scratched	
11 teacher	23 squadron	35 twitch	
12 wand	24 chauvinism	36 archive	

Now use this table to show which part of Unit 5: Common letter patterns can help you.

Mistakes on numbers	Unit 5: Common letter patterns	Activities
2, 3, 7, 8, 11, 20, 21, 26, 27, 34, 35, 42	'ch' and 'tch' words page 58	1, 2
6, 10, 19, 24, 25	'ch' or 'sh' words page 59	Activity (no number)
1, 22, 36, 41	'ch' or 'k' words page 59	Activity (no number)
4, 5, 9, 14, 17, 18, 28, 29, 30, 31, 44	'ou' letter patterns pages 60–61	1, 2, 3
12, 16, 32, 33, 40	'w' letter patterns page 62	1, 2, 3
13, 15, 23, 37, 38, 39, 43, 45	'q' letter patterns page 63	1, 2, 3

Diagnostic test 7: Prefixes and suffixes – Answers

Check your answers against the correct options.

1 unmasked	11 beautiful	21 always
2 undergrowth	12 sharpest	22 misspell
3 preselect	13 fixing	23 unnerve
4 immature	14 battlements	24 illegal
5 rediscover	15 priceless	25 misspent
6 overhead	16 darken	26 overreact
7 misbehave	17 enjoyed	27 immaterial
8 unnatural	18 higher	28 unnoticed
9 antifreeze	19 happiness	29 irregular
10 disallow	20 dreaded	30 immediate

31 darkness	41 forgiveness	51 carrying
32 nightly	42 victories	52 abilities
33 retirement	43 believed	53 slobbish
34 traded	44 carefully	54 wetter
35 demanding	45 forgiving	55 chiselling
36 hopeful	46 easiest	56 travelling
37 exactly	47 clueless	57 homeless
38 winding	48 nursing	58 faithful
39 hardness	49 heaviest	59 spiralling
40 carrying	50 amused	60 grovelling

Now use this table to show which part of Unit 4: Prefixes and Suffixes can help you.

Mistakes on numbers	Unit 4: Section and page	Activities
1–10	Prefixes pages 37–39	1, 2, 3, 4, 5, 6
11–20	Suffixes page 40	1, 2, 3
21–30	Prefixes pages 37–39	1, 2, 3, 4, 5, 6
31–40	Suffixes page 40	1, 2, 3
41, 47, 57	When to keep 'e' page 42	1, 2
43, 45, 48, 50	When to drop 'e' page 43	1, 2
42, 46, 49, 51, 52	Changing 'y' to 'i' page 47	1, 2
53, 54	Doubling pages 44–45	1, 2, 3
44, 58	Suffixes page 40	1, 2, 3
55, 56, 59, 60	'l' rule page 46	1, 2

Diagnostic test 8: Word endings – Answers

Check your answers very carefully against the correct letter patterns.

1 occasion	7 mansion	13 depression	19 tactician
2 electrician	8 magician	14 adoration	20 exhibition
3 acceleration	9 aggression	15 confession	21 optician
4 discussion	10 exclusion	16 beautician	22 potion
5 possession	11 passion	17 physician	23 dimension
6 explosion	12 devotion	18 expansion	24 television

25 nervous	30 advantageous	35 hideous	40 mysterious
26 tedious	31 nutritious	36 anxious	41 spontaneous
27 jealous	32 generous	37 gorgeous	42 simultaneous
28 courageous	33 anonymous	38 monstrous	
29 scrumptious	34 curious	39 poisonous	

43 decimal	49 electrical	55 animal	61 beetle
44 final	50 accidental	56 pedal	62 fiddle
45 bottle	51 ankle	57 diabolical	63 candle
46 purple	52 crystal	58 needle	64 emotional
47 manual	53 arrival	59 miracle	65 mingle
48 giggle	54 financial	60 logical	66 mechanical

67 indicate	72 irritate	77 eradicate	82 participate
68 opposite	73 invite	78 celebrate	83 demonstrate
69 imitate	74 decorate	79 alternate	84 evaporate
70 terminate	75 concentrate	80 co-operate	
71 recite	76 granite	81 navigate	

85 musical	90 obstacle	95 icicle	100 chemical
86 medical	91 article	96 mathematical	101 barnacle
87 miracle	92 geographical	97 biblical	102 classical
88 vehicle	93 spectacle	98 tentacle	
89 technical	94 physical	99 comical	

103 innocence	107 audience	111 appliance	115 dependence
104 distance	108 brilliance	112 science	116 insurance
105 coincidence	109 evidence	113 ambulance	117 romance
106 performance	110 experience	114 licence	118 glance

119 acceptable	122 affordable	125 divisible	128 compatible
120 understandable	123 responsible	126 flexible	129 valuable
121 comfortable	124 washable	127 probable	130 legible

Now use this table to show which part of Unit 6: Common Endings can help you.

Mistakes on numbers	Unit 6: Section and page	Activities
1, 6, 7, 10, 18, 23, 24	'-sion' endings page 71	6, 7
3, 12, 14, 20, 22	'-tion' endings page 69	1, 2
4, 5, 9, 11, 13, 15	'-ssion' endings page 70	3, 4
2, 8, 16, 17, 19, 21	'-cian' endings page 71	5, 7
25, 27, 32, 33, 38, 39	'-ous' endings page 67	1, 2
26, 29, 31, 34, 36, 40	'-ious' endings page 68	3, 4
28, 30, 35, 37, 41, 42	'-eous' endings page 68	5
45, 46, 48, 51, 58, 59, 61, 62, 63, 65	'-le' endings page 72	1
43, 44, 47, 49, 50, 52, 53, 54, 55, 56, 57, 60, 64, 66	'-al' endings page 73	4, 5
67, 68, 69, 70, 71, 72, 73, 74, 75, 76, 77, 78, 79, 80, 81, 82, 83, 84	'-ate' and '-ite' endings page 78	1, 2, 3
85, 86, 89, 92, 94, 96, 97, 99, 100, 102	'-ical' endings page 75	1, 2, 3
87, 88, 90, 91, 93, 95, 98, 101	'-icle' and '-acle' endings page 76	4, 5, 6, 7
103, 104, 105, 106, 107, 108, 109, 110, 111, 112, 113, 114, 115, 116, 117, 118	'-ence' and '-ance' endings page 77	1, 2, 3
119, 120, 121, 122, 123, 124, 125, 126, 127, 128, 129, 130	'-able' and '-ible' endings page 74	1, 2, 3

Diagnostic test 9: Letter patterns – Answers

Check your answers very carefully against the correct letter patterns.

(a) (ai) (ay) (ei) (ey) (ea)

1 train	**5** steak
2 stay	**6** manger
3 obeyed	**7** break
4 freight	

(e) (ea) (ee) (ie) (ei) (i)

8 team	**12** meat
9 complete	**13** feet
10 ceiling	**14** Pauline
11 retrieve	

(i) (y) (ie) (ye) (uy) (ey)

15 fine	**19** dye
16 Guy	**20** pie
17 goodbye	**21** type
18 buy	

(o) (oa) (ow) (ough) (ew)

22 toad	**26** float
23 sow	**27** sew
24 slow	**28** dough
25 bones	

(u) (oo) (o) (ew)

29 do	**33** crew
30 June	**34** spoon
31 rude	**35** commuter
32 moon	

(u) (ue) (ew) (eu)

36 Tuesday	**40** ewe
37 tune	**41** neutral
38 pupil	**42** Europe
39 few	

Now use this table to show which part of Unit 2: Vowels and Consonants can help you.

Mistakes on numbers	Unit 2: Section and page	Activities
1, 2, 3, 4, 5, 6, 7	Long vowel sound 'a' page 26	1, 2, 3
8, 9, 10, 11, 12, 13, 14	Long vowel sound 'e' page 27	4, 5
15, 16, 17, 18, 19, 20, 21	Long vowel sound 'i' page 27	6, 7
22, 23, 24, 25, 26, 27, 28	Long vowel sound 'o' page 28	8
29, 30, 31, 32, 33, 34, 35	Long vowel sound 'u' page 28	9, 10
36, 37, 38, 39, 40, 41, 42	Long vowel sound 'u' page 28	9, 10

Glossary

Abbreviation	A word written in a shortened form. For example: **don't** is an abbreviation of **do not**.
Adjective	A word that describes something. For example: red, tall, exciting.
Consonant	All the letters of the alphabet apart from the vowels.
Consonant suffix	A suffix which starts with a consonant. For example: **-ness**.
Compound words	When two or more separate root words are put together. For example: **Foot + ball = football**.
Drafting	The process of checking and proof-reading work to improve it and correct mistakes.
Homophones	Words that sound the same but have different spellings and meanings. For example: **cereal / serial allowed / aloud**.
Infinitive	The most basic form of a verb, with 'to' in front of it. For example: to play, to be, to run.
Irregular plurals	Plurals that are not formed by adding s, or letter combinations including s. For example: **child → children**.
Mnemonic	A rhyme or saying to help you remember a spelling. For example: Sep**arat**e is **a rat** of a word.
Noun	A word that names things. For example: car, worry, table, life.
Plural	A word that indicates there is more than one. For example: cows, pennies, knives.
Pronoun	A word used instead of a noun. For example: it, he, she, we, they.

Proper noun   A noun which names something specific.
For example: Andrew, France, September. Proper nouns always have a capital letter.

Prefix   A group of letters added to the beginning of a word which changes the meaning.
For example: **Mis** + understand = misunderstand.

Root   A word to which prefixes and suffixes may be added to make other words.
For example, with unclear, cleared or clearly, the root is clear. It is sometimes called a stem word.

Silent letter   Letters that appear in the spelling of a word but are not heard when the word is spoken:
For example: dum**b**, **k**nee, **w**rong.

Singular   A word that indicates there is only one of something.
For example: cow, penny, knife.

Suffix   A group of letters added to the end of a word which changes the meaning. Understand +**ing** = understanding.

Syllable   Each separate beat or sound in a word.
For example:
chapter = 2 syllables (**chap + ter**);
forgotten = 3 syllables (**for + got + ten**).

Verb   An action or 'doing' word.
For example: frown, punch, stretch, eat.

Vowel   The letters **a**, **e**, **i**, **o**, **u** are all vowels.

Vowel suffix   A word ending which starts with a vowel.
For example: **-ing**.

Heinemann is an imprint of Pearson Education Limited, a company incorporated in England and Wales, having its registered office at Edinburgh Gate, Harlow, Essex, CM20 2JE. Registered company number: 872828

www.heinemann.co.uk

Heinemann is a registered trademark of Pearson Education Limited

Text © Pearson Education Limited 2009

First published 2009

16

10

British Library Cataloguing in Publication Data is available from the British Library on request.

ISBN: 978 0 435 806 26 2

Designed and produced by Ken Vail Graphic Design
Original illustrations © Pearson Education Limited 2009
Illustrations by Phil Healey
Cover design by Ken Vail Graphic Design Limited
Printed in Malaysia, CTP-PJB

Acknowledgments

The authors and publisher would like to thank the following individuals and organisations for permission to reproduce photographs: p9 Franklin; p17 Shutterstock.com/Planner; p24 Haruyoshi Yamaguchi/Corbis UK Ltd; p25 C. Paramount/Everett/ Rex Features; p31 Schlegelmilch/Corbis; p33 (Jamie Oliver) Frantzesco Kangaris/Alamy; p33 (monkey) Sharon Morris/ Shutterstock; p33 (footballers) Matthew Peters/Manchester United/Getty Images; p34 Rex Features; p46 Interfoto/ Pressebildagentur/Alamy; p59 Photodisc/Cole Publishing Group/ Bob Montesclaros; p71 Pictorial Press Ltd/Alamy; p76 Photodisc/ Kevin Peterson; p77 Ian Shaw/Alamy; p82 C20th Fox/Lucasfilms/ Ronald Grant Archive; p86 (photos a–e) Clive Andrews.

Every effort has been made to contact copyright holders of material reproduced in this book. Any omissions will be rectified in subsequent printings if notice is given to the publishers.